Usi..g ..
and clear life's pathway to ultimate joy.

Be Light
and Live

The Heavenly Gift

Janet E. Taylor

This method is not just for therapists. Anyone who wants to Be Light and Shine will discover greater clarity and joy as they use this simple, but powerful, method of discovery for healing.

The main focus of this book is that every illness and problem in our body has a beginning, an emotional capstone! This is the object of the Integration work, that through prayer, God will lead one to the deepest capstone, and a new level of health and joy for life may be realized.

~ Janet E. Taylor

Arlene had been a practicing hypnotherapist for ten years. A hypnotherapist helps a person think into the subconscious mind, searching for a solution to an emotional problem they are trying to resolve. The mind will always search backwards, going through life's experiences, to find the very beginning of a core problem. When the body and mind unwind from the core to the present time, there is a tremendous, positive change in the person being worked with.

When the concepts of Be Light *Clear-ology* were presented to Arlene, at first she was mystified. She had to refer constantly to the tracking chart to understand the direction of thought for the process. Now she finds she has a blueprint to logically track to core energy. In her earlier method, she had only explored the surface and recent manifestations of the problem.

Arlene recognized that once she was cleared through *Clear-ology* with the Be Light method and Integration, she was more clear and found new levels of understanding, not just with herself, but for others. She was more balanced and knew there were deep releases in her core energy.

Using the new and easier tracking method, Arlene noticed her clients had more thorough, faster and more complete results.

She was pleased with how the layers peeled away rapidly and methodically, reaching the very core.

Arlene's business has grown as satisfied clients told others about it. Word of mouth of her thoroughness and results is better than a flier or advertisement.

The steps for **_Clear-ology_**, tracking and using the Integration are in the Resources section of this book.

Be Light and Live – The Heavenly Gift
©2004 Janet E. Taylor

ISBN-13: 978-1516804580
ISBN-10: 1516804589

First Edition: July 2017
Second Edition: September 2017

Dedication

While writing this book, my family felt neglected because of the time spent away from them. But every moment, breath, and thought was for them. My youngest daughter said,

"When you speak, it echoes down the hallway. When you write, it echoes through the ages."

My love for them is "Eternal"...that they may , "Be Light and Live".

To my children with love.

To my grandchildren and great grandchildren with love

To those yet to come, this is my legacy.

Contents

Part One: Then

Part Two: Now

Authors Comments and Personal Story

Resources

Be Light Community

Samples

Your Gifts

About the Author

Forward

I am excited to finally see Janet's book in print. Janet Taylor is considered a sage in the healing communities because she is continually improving her trade, learning/applying new modalities of healing such as cranial therapy, hypnotherapy and MNLP (Master Neuro Linguistic Programming)) and sharing her wisdom with others.

I met Janet twenty years ago when I was referred to her for a healing treatment. Janet has kept my family and friends out of crisis many times over the years as she turned complicated signs of distress into simple healing and personal growth.

Be Light and Live contains Janet's applied wisdom and research and is written for the seasoned healer with experience in energy healing, as well as the layperson.

Janet explains that we are more than a physical body. We are eons of ancient energy loaded with deep inner programs, most of them perceptions that hold us from self-discovery, love and forgiveness of the self and others. In Be Light and Live there is an easy tracking method that will identify these problems and release them.

I have never worked with someone more caring than Janet. Each client is a personal connection and this shows up in her book as she uses fictional characters to portray important human connections and healing.

Susan Z. Mackert, MEd

Acknowledgements

Wonderful friends gave me their time, talents, and knowledge. I am very grateful and thankful that they care, love, and accept me as I am. I have had trials and they nurtured me, keeping me on track to edit and finish the manuscript.

Jeanette read and typed the hand-written pages for days. She actually created the beginning of the book as it was to become. One spring day she said, "Deciphering your hieroglyphics is getting easier! Do we now have what you really want to say?"

Raeone helped structure the main body of the book and taught me more steps on how to use my computer. She became exceptional at sorting out my thoughts, making two paragraphs out of an already edited page. It took endless typing to get the story and work understandable.

How exciting to have formatted pages blended and clarified by Diana. A year and a half of work actually began to look like a real book.

The other helpers are SherLynne, Lyn, Brad and Mona. These wonderful souls believe in the blend of prayer and its integration into the story. The gratitude I feel is enormous!   The many hours they have unselfishly spent for Heavenly Father, humanity, the Book, and me is so appreciated. I say to them: "THANK YOU!"

With many needed visuals and hands-on explanations in order to understand the process, the 'Integration' became effective not only by me but also by those who helped me. Because of the faithful dedication of my wonderful friends, they have given themselves and the world "A Heavenly Gift of Light" and they Shine.

The Mission

By blending the Integration and prayer,
Life's confusions will evolve into
Positive self-development,
Personal growth,
And a monumental feeling of joy,
Inner peace and tranquility
May the world "Be Light".

Introduction

In December of 2002, Spirit spoke to me and said, "Write a book!" My Heavenly Guides have great faith in me. With fear and trepidation, I got started. I did not write well, but writing has become a learned ability. The work that I completed each day was written in long hand, then each page was placed in a small basket. It wasn't long before I had a nice pile of completed pages. This was the beginning.

There have been, non-stop, Prayers and Clearings for this book. The word, Clearology, came to me as being clear with my Father in Heaven because His infinite acceptance and connection to me was everything. This book is for Him to use as He sees fit. It is information about the "Integration" as it has changed and developed and as He has clarified my thoughts in the process.

I have written most of the text in story form. The story and characters are fiction. But I write from true life experiences woven into the plot, so that I get my thoughts on paper for others to have more 'Light' in their lives. This process of work has been major for me, for it quickly clears negative energy from the physical, emotional, and mental. It blends all into the spirit, uniting the physical or flesh into wholeness. It addresses ALL of the energy in personal creation, even to point Zero of Infinity, the physical DNA, emotional, mental, spiritual energy, 12 chakra energy centers, dimensions, universes, other worlds, and all of the Divine Intelligence of the Sub-conscious to the beginning point of our own creative powers.

What is the Gift

- The Light of God represents joy, happiness, and a state of peace.
- The Gift is to be a positive clearing for God, all energy becoming its highest dimensional frequency possible.
- It easily erases all kinds of negative energy, thus empowering you to become your very highest in emotional, mental, and spiritual strength.
- Releasing God's children from the myriads of DNA programs gifted to them by their progenitors, we get to keep the good programs and erase the bad ones!
- Because of the desire to improve, we will change negative into positive. The Christ consciousness makes our energy clear and "Light ".
- By energy osmosis, one positive person will create change that may influence 20,000 souls around him or her.
- We will be better today than we were yesterday because of God, Prayer and the Integration. This is the work and the Gift.
- By Prayer and the Integration, Light and Love is what you get to be.

- Through this book, the "LOVE of GOD" is recognized deeply in our cellular core energy.
- As you become the "LIGHT AND LOVE OF GOD" upon the earth, YOU are "THE GIFT!"

Part One

Then

Illya and the King

I llya had just climbed the long spiraling staircase to the top landing of the tower. She loved the solitary, peaceful feeling of a high lofty post. Her legs felt weak and shaky and her breathing came in quick, deep puffs from the exertion. She bent over with her hands on her knees, drawing in deep breaths to recover her strength. As she raised her head and looked around, she was awestruck, as usual. She loved this beautiful, favorite spot. It always made her feel thankful to be alive.

Beautiful green Ivy grew up the wall and formed an arch around the curved windows of the Castle Tower. The flowers and berries of the ivy attracted bluebirds. She often felt and could imagine she was in a forest. She always looked forward to being up away from the business and work of everyone in the castle.

As she stood looking out the window from the highest level of her castle home, a sprig of Ivy, pushed by the breeze, tickled her arm.

A bluebird came to rest on the rock window ledge beside her. It cocked its little head as though to say, "This is my space, but we can share it if you like." She said to the little bird, "Do you feel free little bird? Do you find time for yourself? I do not. It is always, 'Princess Illya this. Princess Illya that.' What am I to do little bird? Can you tell me how to handle all the tasks that I have to do?"

The little bluebird, twitching its tail, became nervous and flew away. She watched it go, flying a swooping circle, and then it landed back on the windowsill, but farther away from her this time. She said, "Little bird enjoys freedom," and she took crumbs from her pocket and placed them on the ledge for the bird.

The heavy responsibility of organizing and helping prepare the food, plus keeping the castle beautiful and clean, required perseverance and fortitude. She was constantly asked what to do, when, how, and where to do it until her head thumped. She yearned to let her youthful spirit enjoy the freedom of being young. She longed for the self-reliance and confidence she had when her Mother was alive. Now she could only find peaceful harmony in this tower when she took a break to be with the birds, the ivy, and always the memory of her Mother.

She gazed into the sky where large fluffy clouds were gathering and the setting sun made the clouds gilded and electric, every swirl of fluffy white exuded gold around the edges. She was fascinated with each shape of the huge puffs and concentrated on the outline of a perfect lamb that even had ears and a tail. Slowly, the evening breeze made it diminish and fall apart. An ear floated away, then the tail was gone. Taking a deep breath, she closed her eyes and felt the peace quietly pulling her back together, buoying her up, and giving her strength.

At age eighteen she was very much like every other young woman. Here in the tower she could be what she wanted to be. Often by imagining, she could pretend to be older, grander, more beautiful, conversant, and more graceful than she really was. With her hand in the air, bent at the wrist, she turned to the little bird pointing her little finger out and up, pretending that the little blue bird was a handsome prince.

The prince had impeccable manners, and he had come to save her from all her problems. Because of her charisma, he carried her off on his white stallion, clamoring to kiss her hand and adore her. He honored her magnificent smile and sought her warm and sweet affections. She closed her big brown eyes and threw her dark head back all the way, feeling the warmth of the sun and imagining what it would be like to be kissed by a suitor.

Here in her private domain, she felt as free as the birds who shared the space. She was especially peaceful at this moment and felt free to enjoy the view of the valley below. She could see the entire kingdom from her stone-walled windows in the tower.   This was the highest elevation in the castle. No one came here and no one knew where she was. It was the way she wanted it to be.

However Aka, her little brother, somehow always knew where she was. She did not mind when he came to find her.

However, this was her private reward when duties were finished for the day or any other time when she felt she needed it. She came here only once or twice a week.

Illya`s hands and arms rested on the rock windowsill. The coolness of the stones filled her with a sense of belonging. Her thoughts went to her past.

She had lived in the kingdom's castle with her parents for as long as she could remember. How blessed she felt to have a wonderful father who was King of the land. Her mother was sweet, kind, and very organized; but God had needed her. She had passed to the Great Beyond after a short, but terrible illness. Now Illya's heart ached with loss and loneliness.

Her life had changed dramatically. She was now filling her mother's position in the castle. She continued to gain even more expertise, making her more proficient. For a castle to function smoothly was a practiced, studied art. Illya felt it had been hard to learn all her mother's skilled duties and do them with her mother's efficiency. She had made many mistakes, but not having a mother to turn to was forcing her to grow up fast. She was accepting responsibility far beyond her age. She had learned to make decisions quickly. Now, a year had passed and everything was flowing smoother. Some of the duties were a joy because they reminded her of her dear mother and kept the love within her heart alive.

Time was passing too quickly since her mother had gone. Illya often found herself pondering the beautiful expressions of love, and tenderness that belonged only to her mother. She so wanted to remember and never forget.

Illya had good artistic ability because she had been learning to draw since a child. She had her materials with her today. She was trying to capture her mother's finer features so she would never forget them. This was important to her. She was frustrated because her inability to draw perfectly could cause those beautiful memories to fade and be lost forever. She longed for the memory of her mother's face and sweet personality to remain strong and preserved, forever! Her worry was that those memories were fading all too rapidly.

The kingdom had grown safer, larger, and dearer to her in a few short years; or perhaps it was that she was now old enough to see more clearly and recognize the growth. It was amazing to notice how many homes filled the beautiful, oval-shaped valley. And more buildings were springing up in the distance. As some people left, others came and filled the empty spaces as if directed by the light of her beautiful valley.

As she gazed out over the basin, she noticed rising tendrils of smoke from family fires used to prepare the evening meal. It was a beautiful evening with very little daylight left. She stood and enjoyed the view. She let her whole being feast on the expanse below, searching as far as she could see.

She could hear a cow low to her calf as though calling it to dinner. The calf answered back with a bahaa. A horse whinnied as a reminder that he wanted his dinner also.

The clouds were especially golden in the fading light over the watering well that was close to the front gate of the castle. The gate stood open, guarded with a few sentries. She remembered when the gates had to always be closed and guarded carefully with many sentries.

This was the gathering place for the village, and it was busy at this time of evening. Illya, unobserved in her tower, watched as women and children came to collect not only fresh water, but also information. It was the place to visit and exchange recipes and news.

She watched as the many wooden buckets were dropped into the well, and imagined the splash as the buckets hit the water some distance below. Then, the full buckets were raised, assisted by ropes being pulled hand over hand with the assistance of an "A" frame and pulleys above the well. When the swinging bucket reached the rock wall circling the well, the water was poured into earthenware pots or jugs and carried to the homes. This was a daily process. It amazed her how strong the women were as they carried the liquid treasure on their heads or with hooks that consisted of a piece of wood carved to fit their shoulders. Two hooks secured the jugs, one each end. These heavy, full jugs rocked back and forth, spilling some of their treasure on flowers, as the women walked slowly to their homes. Those who had been patiently talking and laughing while waiting for their turn took the empty space. This process continued until it was too dark to see. As she watched the activity below, her heart filled with love for her people, for they loved this land as did she. "How strong and well they are!" she commented to the little bird.

She looked at the craggy, snowcapped mountains which surrounded the valley. Gentle forested slopes fell away to meet the groomed fields of golden grain. The waning sun would soon set beyond the mountains to the west. She noticed the long shadows cast across the valley floor from the clouds and trees. The cool gentle breezes were descending into the valley, a welcome change from the heat of the afternoon.

She could hear the rhythmic chorus of cricket's from the hillside. Their song added to the stillness of this peaceful evening. It was as though they were singing to the first stars that were just now coming into view. This added to the light of a new moon peeking over the horizon. The stars and the moon would soon illuminate the basin below. The view warmed her heart.

She noticed that the little bluebird was still there, watching her. She felt in her pocket for the bread crumbs she had brought from the kitchen and laid them on the windowsill. She watched the nervous little bird eat them. She sighed with happiness and gratitude and felt restored and strengthened from her rest and feeding the birds.

Illya, at eighteen, was twice the age of her brother, Aka. When Illya had been nine her mother, Enya, placed the newborn Aka in her arms. She had felt grown up holding him. Instantly, he had reached up, wrapped his tiny fingers around one of hers and pulled it hungrily into his mouth. As he chewed and sucked on her finger, a massive feeling of motherly instinct swept over her. At this young age, she felt herself becoming powerfully and lovingly bonded to him. She had vowed, "I will love you and care for you, forever, my baby brother."

She realized with a feeling of deep affection what a miracle this bonding was. God was in charge and had known their future. Now, she had become his second mother. She knew a mother's love was necessary for her brother to be whole and happy. He depended on her, and she liked his dependence. She was there for him daily, and she would keep her promise to him the rest of her life and forever, if needed.

She smiled and remembered when the cook's daughter made fun of him. He had run to Illya, crying. She had soothed him and then chided, "You are Prince of this land. All of the kingdom will be yours, and you will govern it one day. You must rise above the rudeness of others and remain fair and kind."

"He is a handsome young man," she thought. "With his dark hair and wide set eyes, broad shoulders and narrow hips, he will grow to be a wonderful, strong, striking man. Father will need his army to keep the admiring young women away." Her heart melted. "I love him as God loves me."

She took a deep breath and threw her head and arms back as a gentle breeze whispered through her long, shiny, dark tresses. Her small oval face had large almond shaped, brown eyes with long thick black lashes fringing her rosy cheeks. Her small mouth, white beautiful teeth and a sweet smile on her delicate pink lips made her look fragile and delicate.

She stretched her arms straight to her sides and shook her strong, slender, petite body. Her small feet tapped out a swaying dance as she thought of music that she loved. "Yes, bluebird," she said, smiling a sweet full-lipped smile. "Aka will be a big man. I am sure Aka will not be small like me; I am small like my mother. This makes me happy, but perhaps I will grow more." She stretched her slender arms up over her head again and waved them back and forth in the air as her feet tapped out the imaginary music. It felt good to stretch and sway. She extended her arms as far as she could reach, waving and rolling her hands as she hummed a tune. She did this to the same rhythm of the tune running through her mind.

The little bluebird cocked his head sidewise to watch her with one eye, then hopped a small distance away as if he was skeptical of her unusual movements.

Aka

Aka slowly and laboriously climbed the 350 steps of the tower staircase. He was looking for his sister. He had looked everywhere for her. He missed her, but his guess was she had gone where she always went when she came up missing. When they both were younger, she would carry him to the tower. He felt certain he would find her there. He was almost too tired to finish the climb. "Why does she always come up here?" he asked himself.

Finally, he was at the top landing of the stairs. He saw Illya by the rock window. Her hands were in the air and her body was making strange movements! "Hmm," he thought. "That bluebird hopping around and fluttering its wings seems to be doing the same thing as Illya! Oh, no! They are dancing! Hee hee," Aka giggled.

Quietly, on tiptoe with his hand over his mouth to stifle the chuckles that squeaked out between his fingers, he crept silently up behind her, jumped at her, poked her in the ribs, and exclaimed, "Boo"! She jumped with pretended shock, quickly turned, and put her arms out to him in a gesture of acceptance. "Aka! I wondered if you would find me!"

He joined her with a hug and tried to see what she was looking at. Even on his tip toes, he was not tall enough to see anything but the edge of the windowsill. He had his head all the way back and saw only the evening sky with several big fluffy clouds that looked gold around the edges. He was nine, bigger than he used to be but not tall enough yet. He longed to be a tall, big man like his father. Illya used to lift him to the windowsill to look at the valley below. However, she could not do it now; she was not strong enough as he was too big. "Oh well," he thought. "I'll get that chair to stand on."

The chair was large, heavy and wooden. It would solve the problem if he could move it. He grunted and groaned, moving the chair one inch at time. Illya noticed how heavy the chair was and helped him.

Now Aka jumped up on the chair so he might see what Illya was looking at. She stood with her arm around her little brother's waist. He was now slightly taller than she was. He looked down on the top of her head and pretended they were the same age; only he was big now, all grown up! He liked that macho feeling of finally being bigger. He wanted to be stronger and pretended that he was caring for her. Feelings of love flooded over him *"I will take care of you, my sister, and love you forever,"* he said to himself.

Softly she whispered to Aka, "Listen to the song of the crickets. Did you notice the gold lining on the clouds? Look at the candles glowing like lights in every window in our village. They look like different sized stars that have fallen to the earth and entered each home but are still shining so we can see them this evening.

"Aka, always remember that you and I belong together." Illya and Aka turned and looked deeply into one another's eyes, feeling the bond. "Yes", they each thought and then said out loud at the same time,

"We are family, and we belong together forever."

Illya continued to think as she and Aka gazed out of the tower window. "Yes, " she thought. "I am very happy that I have Aka, but I miss the companionship of my mother. There are many things I would ask her and learn from her.

" One is never prepared for the loss of a loved one."

Only two years before, the Kingdom had been in chaos, horrible things had taken place. It had been unsafe for Illya or Aka to leave their castle home and walk the streets in the city, as they now do. Often when Illya looked from the upper window before this last year, she could witness unjust things taking place but could do nothing about it. She had wept because of what she saw and the hopelessness she felt. She thought about her father and the great love that he always gave to his people by being fair and kind in his judgments. This chaos seemed so wrong.

Parel

Illya remembered when she had gone to find her father in his courtroom. Across the courtyard, she witnessed a woman being ushered to her father for judging.

How could one forget the dark, long, curly hair because most hair in the kingdom was dark and straight? The woman stirred her memory. Who was she?

As she crept close, she recognized her. It was Parel! She had served her mother as a tailor. What was she doing in this court? Surely, Parel would not break the law. All who knew Parel, including her children, respected her. Is it possible that someone so fine had broken the law?

Illya slipped into the back of the room and stood partially hidden behind a large vase. From there she could watch and listen to the proceedings and be unobserved.

Illya knew the court was for those who had broken the law. The law required exacting penalty for each crime. The sentenced could lose their life or any number of fingers or even a hand for stealing. It depended on the severity of the crime. They were labeled and had to wear a banner saying, "THIEF". This was ruthless for they must wear this wherever they went for the rest of their lives.

Cℨ

The prosecutor began. "This woman took bread from the Bread Shoppe. Whoever represents the Shoppe and caught this thief, please come forward."

The bread maker of the Shoppe stepped forward. "I saw this woman as she took the bread," he said. "I knew she was not going to pay for it because she tried to run away. I caught her, and now I want her to pay for this crime."

"Does this man tell the truth?" the King asked.

"Yes," Parel admitted. "My children were hungry. For several days there had been no food for them to eat. I needed food! I could not bear to see them hungry another day. My husband died as a guard for the castle. The money he left me is gone. It has been one year since the loss of my tailor position at the castle and two years since the loss of my husband. I have worked hard. I did sewing for Queen Enya; but since her death, I cannot find enough work to care for my family. There is no longer food in my home and no money to buy any." With this admission, Parel began to sob.

Illya observed her father's reaction as his heart swelled with compassion. She knew he wanted to help Parel, not hinder her.

The King was touched by Parel's straight-forward confession and had been trying to recall who this woman was. When she mentioned Queen Enya, a memory of all the beautiful gowns she had created for his deceased wife and daughter came to his mind. Her dark, unusually beautiful curly hair helped him remember the many times he had observed her serving his wife. There was no one in the kingdom that had hair like Parel. How had he overlooked not having this good person working in the castle?

He realized that in his state of grief and anguish at not wanting to accept Enya's death, he was overlooking many things pertaining to his loving wife. He thought of Parel in a kindly way; for he realized she was a friend of his wife, not just the seamstress who sewed her clothing.

He also knew honesty is a choice of the very moment.

Parel had failed to make the right decision. He wanted to be gentle with her but at the same time, also uphold the laws of the kingdom. He had to punish her because the law of the land bound him, and she had transgressed. But what would it be like to have hungry children? There would have to be something as devistating as crying, hungry children for Parel, in desperation, to do something like this to feed them. She must have been frantically in need, as he knew her to be honest, trust worthy, and capable.

"Parel, you have broken the law and must surely be punished. I cannot change the law for you or anyone else. You have told me the truth and I understand your need for food, but you must never break the law again!

"Any little dishonesty is a large problem. Your word is your honor.

"I am sorry, but you must still be punished." Parel knelt before the king and answered ashamedly, "I make a vow this day to be honest in word and deed. I choose, never again to be an example of dishonesty.

*"This feeling of dishonor is **worse than the feeling of hunger.**"* Parel said.

Illya could feel the reluctance of her father, the King, to maim this poor woman. He was compassionate and kind; he governed his kingdom with unconditional love. However, this woman was not the usual dishonest thief and troublemaker.

He arose from his throne and went to the person who stood ready to inflict the punishment. He spoke in a whisper, "Cut only the skin on the end of the little finger on her left hand; and the banner, **Thief**, will be worn for two weeks."

Then the King sent a messenger to the Overseer of the castle instructing him to have Parel do the washing and ironing of the linens of the castle. He also requested her to sew clothing for himself and Aka, and dresses for Illya. *This would allow Parel to be home with her three children as a devoted mother.* This new position would provide food and clothing for her family.

He also created a pension for all castle help who had lost a mate while employed by the King. He arranged for the oldest boy of Parel to be an apprentice to the shoemaker in the village. Together, Parel and her oldest child would provide adequately for the family without more poverty.

Illya rejoiced as she heard her father make these positions available for Parel's family. Illya knew her father grieved over the crime level of the Kingdom. What would have become of our beautiful land without the changes that have taken place?

Father had to judge all those who did steal, lie, murder, or maim. She knew he longed for this wickedness to stop. He always said in a worried voice, ***"These outward crimes are the actions of the inward desires of a person's heart."***

How can we help those in our kingdom make the changes in their **hearts** that **truth** and **honor** are foremost in every mind? How can we create these actions for everyone in the land?" Father knew to have integrity and love, one must have **Faith** in **God**. This faith would restore truth, and bring peace, joy and happiness back into the hearts of the people. Her father made this part of every prayer and labored unceasingly, teaching this message to all in the kingdom in whatever way he could. A few accepted what he said. But there were those who hardened their hearts and did not respond to the message.

This was tiring for her Father, as she knew he wanted the best for every person.

Slowly Illya's thoughts returned to the present time. "Thank you, God," she murmured. "Thank you for changing our world." She stood silently with her arms around her little brother and felt safe in her high, peaceful tower. She thanked God with a prayer in her heart for the peace and safety with which they were now blessed.

The Journey

Illya remembered when the change began two years ago when she was sixteen years old. There was much disruption in the kingdom, and it seemed Father was always in the courtroom. Being a prayerful person, he prayed to be agreeable with God. When Illya walked by his private room in the castle during what was supposed to be his free time, she found him pondering about his people. It took great courage to issue ultimatums for those who had broken the law. She felt bad for him because he had so little time to spend with her and the royal family. This caused him unhappiness. He lamented the loss of her mother. She could sense his weariness.

When the burden grew too heavy and the need for change was strong, the King would say," Let's go visit our family." They would prepare to be gone for two weeks. Father said," ***A change is as good as a rest.***"

Illya and Aka`s cousins lived in a village two days from the castle. This is usually where they would go for a rest. Father enjoyed visiting with their uncle and aunt. His brother was a governor over a portion of the kingdom under the king's authority. They lived in a spacious home much like a castle. Her father and his brother enjoyed each other very much. The talk and laughter was endless, mainly reliving their boyhood pranks.

The cousin Aka played with was one year older than he was. His name was Amada. Illya noticed that Amada was very much like her father, not only in looks, but also in actions. Amada had a giving heart; he had given Aka a bow with arrows, which Aka would take home with him. Illya decided that there would be some new rules for Aka and his new bow and arrows. Aka was always outside shooting his arrows at anything he could find until Uncle Jared fixed a bull's eye on a roll of straw for him to bury each arrow in as he used it for a target. By the time they returned home, Aka was handling his bow and arrows quite expertly.

Auler was the cousin Illya loved. The girls were very much alike and the same age. They played games, giggled and talked about boy attractions and the joys of growing up. This was the only time she had the enjoyment of being with another girl her age who lived in similar circumstances. Illya's aunt and her mother had been very strong friends. Illya felt sad for her aunt, and was sure her aunt missed her mother.

Family love is first formed in heaven and is the greatest bond on earth.

The companionship of close family is a treasure of love to draw upon for strength and courage.

℘

Father felt that two weeks was a good length of time to visit.

He said a longer visit was like old fish that had lost its freshness.

He always wanted their visits to be enjoyable and fresh. The journey home was two days' travel. It was during the return journey that Illya's life would change forever.

On the second day of their journey, they had been traveling for several hours and had just crossed the border of her uncle's domain. They were still many hours away from their castle home. Aka was admiring and playing quietly with his new bow and arrows. Father, as usual, took this to be a quiet time for sleep and very little conversation.

ＣＺ

THE JOURNEY HOME

The warmth of the day and the jostling and rumble of the coach had lulled Illya to sleep. The horses were steamy from the heavy pull of the coach, sweat coursed down their backs in streams. Illya was jarred awake when the carriage went over a large bump. Jerked to an upright position, she almost hit her head on the ceiling. The carriage was hot and airless. She wanted a cool, fresh breeze on her face so she reached across the carriage and opened the window. That was when it happened! As she leaned forward to let the breeze cool her face, she saw a man's body lying at the edge of the road. She screamed, "Father! Stop the carriage! Someone is hurt! Stop!"

"Stop! Stop! Stop now!" he commanded. The speed of the horses and momentum of the carriage took them down the road some distance before coming to a stop.

Illya bounded through the door of the carriage before it came to a complete stop and ran back to the injured man. "This man must have been hit by an earlier carriage and was left beside the road," she thought. "Who would do this? Who would be so horrible as to run over a man and leave him injured to possibly die?"

The man was in terrible condition. His limbs were broken as bones were protruding through the skin on his arms. His head and neck were in an abnormal position, and blood was streaming from his left ear and nostril. His eyes were closed tightly as if he was enduring the pain. There was a puncture opening in the upper left side of his neck. His breathing sounded restricted as he labored to get air into his lungs. The breath was sucking in through the puncture injury that had possibly severed his breathing tube.

She felt helpless. There was nothing she could do. Nothing! A gurgling sound came from the opening in his throat. Then his breathing stopped! The eyes remained closed and it seemed all of his bodily functions ceased.

Just then, Illya saw a body begin separating from the one on the ground. This body had no weight. There was no evidence of injuries. First, the head, then the rest of the body from the neck down to the feet, lifted out. His eyes were still closed. As he floated free from the body on the ground, he rolled over on to his stomach as he emerged. He pushed himself forward with his arms toward Illya. He looked just like the body on the ground, only he was darker in color.

He definitely had his own agenda; for as he went past Illya, he went partially through her left shoulder. Even though his eyes were closed, he knew where he was going and how to get there.

She noticed the strong odor of wine. "Had he been drunk?" she asked. "Did he lose his life because of it?"

He floated in a horizontal position, still with his eyes closed until he stopped in the middle of the road. It seemed as though he was in a separate space reserved only for him. Even with his eyes closed, he seemed to know exactly where he; was and he knew when to stop. He hovered horizontally, three or four feet above the ground, then he slowly came to an upright vertical position. He was fully clothed and approximately one foot above the road. It was as though he was standing on an unseen platform or on some kind of density that was not physical.

With his eyes closed, he comfortably yawned, gave his mouth a pat and then put his arms out wide and stretched. Then his eyes popped open. He looked around as though he was waking up for the first time. He saw Illya looking at him. The connection between them was clear. No words were spoken, yet a vibrant understanding of every thought and feeling was joined by the synergy of the bond between them.

Illya engaged wholly in the circumstances of the moment and noticed everything about him. The clothing on his new body, the colors, shapes, brightness, every movement, and all inflection was monumentally recorded in her mind.

The clothing on the weightless body was darker in color as though the brightness of the colors was lost, being covered with some strange substance. This dark flat, fluffy cloud-like residue was all over him and about two inches thick. It looked like dark cotton picked from a dark gray cotton plant. This matter kept the true, brighter colors hidden.

Then, as he began to move, the dark residue of cotton began falling from him. He grimaced as if it was a vulgar, nasty mess. He brushed vigorously with his hands, slapping and waving as it fell by dark fluffy, flat, irregular, thick gluey pieces to the area around him. It fell from his hair, body, arms, and legs until it formed a fifteen inch pile around him and came up to his knees.

With the gray residue gone, the colors of his clothing were now brighter, clearer, and stronger than on the dead, earthly body. *The bright, exquisite, stunningly clear colors had always been there, waiting to shine with the grimy darkness gone.*

Illya and the man communicated in their minds. "What is going on here?" he asked.

Illya thought to him, "You were hit by a carriage. You just died, and you are now in a different space."

He looked down at his lighter body, compared himself to the body on the road, and answered, "I'm okay. I am alive." He said this as he touched the chest of his new body with both hands.

He carefully lifted each foot high as he stepped over and out of the circle of dark, nasty fluff. He grimaced at the dark mess around his feet and lower legs. He did not want the dirty, sticky stuff to get on him again. He liked the true, brighter colors that were shining through.

He folded his arms and leaned against a tree. Suddenly, he realized he was falling through the tree. He was shocked! He threw both arms out as though to catch himself! He immediately sprang forward out of the tree and jerked to a vertical position. Again, he asked, "What is going on here?"

"Your physical body just died. You are a light body now. That is your physical body lying beside the road."

Truth finally resonated! His mouth dropped open in surprise and bewilderment. He was staring at his own body, dead upon the ground. *And yet, he was alive!*

Just then, Illya's father laid his hand on her arm and asked, "Illya, are you okay?"

"I don't know," she said. "I think so."

Father and the driver wrapped the man's body in the carriage blanket and strapped him on the back luggage rack. However, Illya discerned that this same spirit man was sitting beside her father. She was amused that Father did not know he had company on the seat beside him. But she also felt very strange with what she had just experienced. She could not really "see" him, but she knew exactly where he was! She had his position pinpointed as she could smell the wine odor of his breath as it wafted through the inside of the coach in varying degrees, depending on where he was looking. The smell made her feel nauseated, but no one else seemed to notice. She tried very hard to ignore the fact that, *She knew he was there!*

Her mind began sorting through this experience. She would never forget it!

She remembered Father teaching at one time during dinner about the Spirit of man being as a light body. He told Aka and her that the spirit body is born a child of God in a pre-existent state where it resided with God, our Eternal Father, and Heavenly Mother. Father taught them that the physical body houses the Spirit. It enters sometime before or during birth. He explained that a Spirit body is more refined and of a purer element than the physical body. This same Spirit enters and lives within the physical body and gives it life. In the physical, it becomes the child born of earthly parents; but a person then has a dual identity. Everyone lives as a dual being, an immortal Spirit body clothed with a body of flesh and bone. The Spirit and the Body constitute the mortal soul.

Father explained, "When we die, our spirit body leaves and goes back to Heaven. Our earthly body stays behind and is buried in the ground.

"A spirit can live independently of the physical body, but the physical body cannot live independently of the spirit".

Thus, Illya understood from her father's teachings that her spirit would live forever, eternally with God the Father.

Illya's mind kept churning, "One day after death, at a time chosen by God, the graves of all who are dead will open and all will be resurrected and purified. The physical body becomes immortal as it unites with the spirit, never to die again. God our Eternal Father is a resurrected, immortal perfect Being. This means alive, but changed, with a more pure immortal substance than blood flowing in the veins and arteries. He is perfect and eternally loving. He is the Father of our spirits."

She decided, "This man is now a spirit. Evidently, my eyes were changed into spiritual eyes so that I could see his spirit. Why, was I gifted to see him?"

She was pondering upon that when her father touched her. His touch pulled her from the spiritual space, and she could not see the man. But she could still smell him and feel his energy. He was indeed present. This odor of wine belonged to *him*!

When they arrived at the next village, they went directly to the authorities. There they learned that the dead man's name was Derth. Derth's wife was due to deliver their third child. They assessed that Derth was a good man who loved his family. He had worked most of the night at the loading docks in the neighboring village. He apparently stopped after work to have a glass or two of wine. He was walking home to his family when the carriage hit him from behind, and he lost his life.

Illya, Aka, and her father visited Derth's home where they met his wife and two adorable children. When she was told of her husband's death, she collapsed in tears. She was soon to deliver another child. What would this poor family do? Illya was glad there were other members of the family there to comfort her. This was a nice family. What would the future hold for them?

She overheard her father arrange for the family's welfare with not only money but also food and provisions. When this was finished, they continued on their homeward journey. Illya felt deep gratitude for her father, the King. "What a wonderful caring heart. I love him so much," she thought.

Learning and Growing

For the entire rest of the journey home, Illya's mind spun with innumerable questions. Did she really see Derth's spirit leave his mortal body? Who would understand that she saw Derth die and yet still talked to him? What would people think if she told them this story? Would they believe her? Would they think she had gone mad? Should she have been able to do something for him?

Her mind would not stop thinking about the experience! She could not believe it was real, could she? The shock of watching Derth die and the implications of what this meant to his family continued in her mind for days, after they returned home. She spent day after day going over every detail in her mind. She had never seen or experienced anything as *horrible* or anything so *spiritual.* Each step was stamped deep in her memory. She would *never* forget. *Never!*

She felt she had to talk to someone. Maybe that would help slow the incident down in her mind. Could she talk to her father? Yes! She had to talk to Father!

They arrived home; and after dinner, she peeked around the corner. Father was in his office at his desk, deep in thought as usual. She hesitated. Should she interrupt his thoughts? Just as she turned to walk away, he sensed her presence.

"Illya, my love, come in," he said. He stood up and looked at this lovely, sweet, sensitive daughter. His heart felt as though it would burst with love for her. She looked so delicate and small, much like her mother. There were times he felt Enya incarnated through her. His heart wrenched with the memory and the pain of losing his beloved wife.

He watched Illya's beautiful, petite form move towards him. She was so tiny with small feet and hands. He could understand how some would think her to be 10 or 12 instead of 17 years old. Her dark hair shone in the light and glistened as she moved towards him. He was proud of how she groomed herself. She had cared for her hair by herself since she was six years old. No one else could touch her hair. She said, "NO! I'll do it myself!" He was amazed at how long it had grown. It was now below her hips. He wondered what it would feel like having hair to sit on. Would it be slippery or does it hurt? Immense love welled in his chest. Tears gathered in his eyes as he held his arms out to his beautiful daughter.

Her eyes smiled into his warm brown eyes. "She has my eyes," he thought as she came into his arms. "Hello, precious," he said as he enfolded her.

He felt her small body trembling. What was wrong? Had something happened to her?

"Father," she said, "I must talk to you. Please may I have some time?"

He remembered she had been unusually quiet and reserved at dinner. Aka, on the other hand, had babbled like a magpie. Dinner was the King's time with his family. He let only an emergency interrupt this special time with them. They always exchanged conversation at the table, reviewing all that had taken place during the day. He loved this time. He enjoyed talking with his children and kindly teased them until they laughed with merriment. The sweet expressions on their faces as they chatted back and forth warmed his heart.

A concerned expression came over his face as he thought again of her silence since their return trip. Illya had been troubled about something.

"Father, I can't seem to calm my mind. I keep going over every detail of the death of Derth. I see the blood and the broken bones in my mind, repeatedly. However, Father, I also saw something else. I need to tell you what I saw and hope you will understand and accept what I tell you as truth and not think me crazy."

Then Illya poured out her story to her father. She told him all that she had witnessed that day on the road by the carriage. It was a relief when he told her with great consolation and love, that he believed her. Her body went limp, her legs became weak and she almost fell.

Father said, "Illya, there is a way to become peaceful when you are troubled or hurt. Come, my dear, I will teach you of Meditation and Prayer. It is the only way to find peace when your mind and heart are troubled.

℘

MEDITATION AND PRAYER

"First, you imagine a safe place, it could be your room or your own bed. It might be anywhere you feel peaceful and safe. I personally sometimes go to a mountaintop in my mind; or I become one of the clouds, drifting and floating. Others may go to a beautiful meadow in their mind. There may be a stream close by and mountain meadow flowers all around. You can create any place you want in your thoughts.

"You may want to experiment until you find a comfortable, peaceful way to start your meditation. Try different ways until you find your special location that will allow you complete focus. It is important to be comfortable. Lie down or sit comfortably in a chair with your *neck* and head supported.

"Time will pass unnoticed if you are comfortable. If you are uncomfortable that is all you will be able to think about.

"Next, begin breathing deeply. Take the breath in through your nose counting seven. Hold to the count of seven. Then slowly expel out through your mouth to the count of seven-- many, many deep breaths -- and let your mind go blank and inward.

"If you cannot find a peaceful place, visualize and pretend your body is a flower. The center of the flower is in your chest. Concentrate. Let your mind go into the center of the flower as you continue to breathe evenly and deeply. Close your eyes and breathe deeply and steadily. Do not go to sleep, but find your quiet space inside.

"Connect to your Higher Power. I think of the Higher Power as God the Eternal Father. He is a glorified, perfect man who literally is your Father, not of the physical, but of the Spirit within. He knows you and loves you. He is always there for you. His Light is powerful, peaceful, and complete. He loves you unconditionally, with no judgment. His Light comes to you as a round pillar or beam. It comes in to the top of your head, then all the way down through your body to a space below your feet. You can then ask that the gift of this Light be allowed to expand and go outward until it is completely in you, around you, and through you.

"When this connection to God is in place, you may ask questions about your existence and get answers. You may ask to know the source of your pain and ask for a release from it. Give all your troubles and problems to *Him*.   Ask that *He* take them away, or give you the answers to help you understand what you are to learn from them. He will show you the way. He will give you peace, and you will be filled with feelings of love and the knowledge of what to do."

"Father," said Illya, "What is the difference between prayer and meditation?"

"It is **Time,**" *said father.* **"Meditation** is spending *Time* with your Father in Heaven. **Prayer** is instant communication. For example, all day long you may talk to God in prayer as you ask for blessings, seek and listen for answers, and pray for others and yourself.

"Prayer can be a short time. Meditation takes time.

"When you give your troubles to God in prayer, the burden is no longer yours. You instantly feel lighter, and you receive peace. However, we are interesting creatures, Illya.

"We give our troubles to God, asking him to take our burdens to lighten our emotional load. When we worry, which is not the nature of God, we take back what we have given and try to take care of it ourself.

"Come, Illya, pray with me," Father said. As father and daughter knelt, hand in hand, something grand and miraculous happened.

☙

The room began to fill with light. Illya and her father saw a *beautiful shimmering Being in brilliant, transparent light.* The colors of the rainbow -- red, orange, yellow, blue, indigo, purple -- plus gold and vast white light shimmered around and through all of the colors of this *Being. The blending colors of golden* light, radiated into *white light so brilliant that it was brighter than the sun at mid-day. It filled the room with a* feeling of joy that was stunningly peaceful.

The resonance of God's Light was with this beautiful Being. Illya and her father knew they were in the presence of a God messenger, although no words had yet been spoken.

The *Light Being* spoke to them, calling them by name but with no words spoken. "There is a way to release grief, pain, and confusion from the mind and body. It is called **Integration**. You asked to know this, so I have come to teach you.

"*Remember as I speak: 'God is in charge of all that is lasting and   good.' "* Bible, Eph. 5: 9-11

℃

"The top of your head is the Spiritual energy center connecting you to God. The energy centers above the waist are spiritual connections. The energy centers from the waist down have to do with your connections to earth and your personal life. The crotch bonds you to the earth by way of *your pelvis, which is energy center number one.*

"The front seven energy centers unite you to spirit and the present time. The back five energy centers connect you to your *Past Intelligence."*

He continued,

"Humans are not physical beings. They are Intelligent, Spiritual beings having a Physical experience upon the earth.

"We are, in reality, eons old in spirit and energy. We live many personal choices brought forward from many infinite, timeless loops of experience. Each choice you have ever made in your entire existence is *now,* in the present time. It is being recreated as either a light or dark choice for you to gain power over weaknesses for immortality. This information has been locked in the super-conscious, sub-conscious and conscious minds. The lock of forgetfulness has now been loosed. The processes will be revealed that took place in the beginning of your creation. You have been in construction of intelligence and spirit, for eons.

"When you chose to become as God, your spirit was made from the DNA of your Heavenly Father and Heavenly Mother. You then gained a body that your spirit would reside in. Your Intelligence has always been and became your Spirit. Then they came into your Physical. Your charge as a physical God creation is to bring all areas of your creation into wholeness and fill them with the Light of God. Always understand that *God is your main focus*. If in some of your creation you chose darkness and did not find a way to correct it by choosing the Light, you now have the opportunity to do so.

"This life is the time to become exalted with the Light of God." 2 Corinthians 6:2

He continued, "Most people are born with a basic desire to do and be good. Those who do bad are usually trained to be bad or have inherited DNA from their physical parents that basically was dark in its origin. We chose at some point in our creation to help clear the darkness of our DNA and the earth darkness and to have the Light of God present in our lives, always.

"There are negative experiences imposed on us by others that will need to be changed, also. Without these interferences from hurt or past memory, there is a basic feeling from the spirit or core of mankind to be and do good.

"Your Spirit's core energy is the Light of God because He gave you His perfect Spirit DNA. This was chosen by you and Heavenly Father as the blueprint to used be used for your physical body. This beautiful blueprint or core energy, your own personal spirit entices you to do good and always travel toward the Light of God.

"When people make bad choices, they are usually devoid of light or are dark in nature or are evil. Unsorted programs of buried memory can hold people in a state of evil confusion. This is what creates physical pain, sickness, and loss.

"There are many negative thought processes constantly repeated that become patterns in the mind. There is a way to release these negative, repetitive programs;

and as you do, pain is also released because pain is not physical.

"Illya, when you saw Derth die, you saw two energy bodies blended, spirit and intelligence. His spirit lifted from the body with his eyes closed in sleep. His intelligence was locked inside of the spirit and took over the direction that he would go. The sleeping spirit was directed past you and to the middle of the road. Intelligence needs no eyes. It is all feelings and knowing.

"His *Intelligence was directing him from and through the spirit body.*

"His Spirit then woke up but did not know where it was. He had to find his way.

"The intelligence knows all and is all and never sleeps. It is like a recorder, recording the minute instances in picture form of life experiences. The Intelligence is a body of energy. It has shape and form just as you or your spirit do but it is not as dense as the Spirit but connects to the universe in its huge vastness.

"Illya, Derth's spirit was asleep because he had not been awakened in the physical to the Light of God. When the physical is aware of His Light, the life energy or the Spirit will leave the body in an awakened state. In spite of having his eyes closed when he lifted out of his body, Derth's Intelligence did not need eyes but was awake and directed him to exactly where he was to go, and what he needed to do. Intelligence is like this. It is always present, awake and recording whether the physical body or spirit is awake or asleep. It holds a record of all information, both good and bad, of our entire creation not just this life. Obviously, he did not have the **Integration** as his Intelligence and Spirit were not blended but separate entities. The **Integration** blends all areas into miraculous wholeness and spiritual power. When complete, we will be immortal or transformed.

"The second energy body state was when Derth woke up and did not know where he was. He then became blended Intelligence into his spirit body. These two bodies of energy function together within the physical body, like I have said, awake or asleep, but most often they register only in the subconscious and super conscious.

"In approximately the third week of embryo, we receive the Intelligence part of our creation. It is injected in, on or close to, the third cervical of the physical baby's head/ neck. That small embryo cranial is busy building a body, setting up DNA,

chromosomes and genetics. It also now has
Intelligence energy to deal with. Many
become jumbled and are in mass confusion
from this point on.

"The spirit, in the same way, is injected
into the physical body of the mother through
the navel and into the baby. This takes place
sometime during or before birth.

"Think of the intelligence as the
subconscious and super conscious. Think of
it as big, even bigger than your castle, and
your brain has to govern all this energy. The
conscious mind in size is as a tiny point of
your tower. There is a lot going on at the
same time. Both the conscious, subconscious,
body and spirit are being shaped and formed
at the same time. In Derth's death, these two
energy bodies you saw were mystically
together and yet separate."

℃

TWELVE ENERGY CENTERS

The Light Being continued, "Altogether,
there are twelve energy centers either on or
going into the body. The twelve energy
centers make up most of the blended

intelligence of the super conscious and subconscious mind. The energy centers carry the information of your blueprint your body is made from.

"We are not aware of the energy centers because they are registered in the forgetful space of the intelligence. They hold a record of all of the Light and Dark choices we have made in all our creation.

"Each Energy Center has twelve levels of 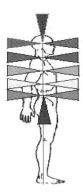 energy called dimensions. They are numbered from One to Twelve. Each one has twelve levels of energy. As you can see, we are very old in our creation.

We have been preparing toward and anticipating completion. We have waited for eons, looking forward to God placing these energy centers to begin your activating experience.

"Inside each center, there are 12 levels, much like plates stacked on top of one another. Each plate is similar to 1,000 years of energy. These need to be cleared of all past negative choices or decisions.

"You exercised your free agency when you chose to become as God our Father.

Thus, locked within each cell in our body is a carbon blueprint of our Father in Heaven's perfection. Because of this, there is an enormous drive to become perfect, always better than we already are.

"In the first twelve days after conception, twelve energy centers as neurons (memories) go into the embryo's memory bank.

"Your brain, now being formed and busy, begins recording the perceptions of embryo life. Recorded are your Mother's and Father's thoughts and feelings, family, where the earth is, and all confusion going on, in, outside, and around the womb.

"For the first sixty days, 200,000 to 500,000 neurons, and sometimes more, are constructed and added daily as genetics to the brain cells. *These neurons build most of the subconscious memory.*

"At this point of development, the embryo and intelligence have completely created the cellular structure of the body, mind and twelve different and individual energy centers as a brilliant whole-brained child of God.

"You are skillfully blending your Intelligence, existence, DNA and genetics. You are also getting ready for that exciting moment when the Spirit will enter. It enters at some time during or before birth, making the body its home, and attaching a spiritual cord for life source through the umbilical cord. This gives the body its own life energy where before it depended on the physical cord of the mother to keep it alive. If the cord for some reason breaks, the baby will die. But the physical body, no matter how big, is claimed as its mortal body.

"After the first twelve days of developmental conception, the neuron creation slows to approximately 100,000 to 200,000 inputs daily until body growth is past five to eight years of age.

"If *trauma* happens, input will speed up again, emblazoning the happening into the brain and sub-conscious memory, never to be forgotten. *But the trauma will create action as a* **perception** *until it is recognized by the conscious mind.*

"The twelve energy centers, when balanced, are naturally spinning to the right. This brings added energy into the body. The energy centers are each shaped like a cone, the tip being a pin dot at the core where it enters into the spinal column. The outer part of the cone extends away from the body in large, outward overlaps with one another.

Each is a different color. This gives a rainbow effect around the body called *Aura Energy*.

"As you become whole with the Light of God, your aura energy becomes perfected and clear and is called "White Light". You want your aura fused with the Light of God because this makes the core energy pure and strong."

"When your aura is fused with the Light of God, it extends outwards a great distance. This affects others for many miles around you. It is like osmosis. This energy is automatically absorbed and transferred by others, bringing all around you to new levels of Light energy. As the level of God energy that *you* are penetrates through the energy that *they* are, the higher level of thinking is automatically accepted by most and lifts all into a new level of light. You alone may affect thousands of people at one time by your level of clearness.

"If you are weak or troubled or think negative thoughts, the aura immediately shrinks and becomes very tight and close around you. A negative aura is charged by negative thoughts that instantly turn the aura black. It will turn red if you are angry, or orange if you need to nurture yourself."

"Your thoughts create what you are and what you have in life. Be careful what you think because you will create it for yourself.

"When you focus on the past, are troubled, ill, or out of balance with life, your energy centers spin to the left. They stop bringing you energy and will turn *counterclockwise.* When you are in this negative state, your energy goes outward away from you and anyone else can claim it. When this energy is going away from you, because of your own thoughts, you become very weak. Energy vampires (those who use and exist on other's energy) may now suck all of your energy out and thrive on it. You become weaker and weaker. This is serious and can cause death."

"What is energy?" asked Illya.

"Energy is never created or destroyed but is only transferred or transformed. It is the ability to produce action or effect. It is strength, force and power. In quantum theory, each nucleus has discrete energy states. In passing from one to another, it sends out gamma rays of sharply defined energy called 'Light'.

"We are on this earth to gain knowledge, use free agency to make positive choices, and become the 'Light of God Energy,' helping ourselves and others to a higher level of Light beingness.

"If you use any product or person to take the place of God in your life, such as marijuana, addictive drugs, alcohol, sex, porn, or any mind-altering product, you are creating a negative spin in your energy. We intermittently change the spin back and forth throughout our life with thought processes. Your spirit/ body creates a positive spin when connected to The Light of God. A positive spin is turning automatically to the right; and when in the Light, you will have energy to live your life with greater power and purpose.

"Learning about the Love of God and letting our life resonate with that complete, unconditional love is what makes all our energy centers balanced.

"I am giving you a 'Gift'. The Gift is called, **'Integration'.** *Use this gift with Prayer.* Never try to use the Gift without prayer.

"The Integration will erase or reverse the negative spin, destroying dark, useless programs and immediately putting you in harmony with God. If you have not been able to pray, this will make it possible for you to pray. The positive spin will then return balance and energy to the body. When there is balance and a positive spin, health and energy abound.

"Information buried in the subconscious mind comes forth as ninety percent of our thoughts and actions in a days' time. It is accessed by thought and acted out through the conscious emotional and mental through actions. This is only ten percent or less of your conscious thinking.

"Most of us use less than ten percent of our conscious mind energy to create experiences, learning, and action in mortal life."

The Light Being continued to explain. "This is how your Body, Mind, Spirit, and Intelligence heal together to full strength, bringing you to your greatest power of good.

"Using your right hand, *tap* one time on the forehead, then tap once on the upper chest just below the neck in the area of the *Thymus gland.*

"The Thymus is the reset button for the body. This will open all twelve energy centers, just like opening twelve doors.

"After the taps with the right hand, *move the same hand over the heart, hold your hand there for just a moment.* This is the reprogram space. This allows you to be free of the past and removes all the layers of bad energy from making wrong choices.

"Placing your *right hand over your heart* gives you the ability to create new programs through positive affirmations. With your right hand over your heart, you will now verbalize affirmations beginning with the terms I AM, I DO, I CHOOSE.

"When used with *prayer* and *meditation, the Integration* will allow a person to reach a more perfect state in this lifetime.

"The sub-conscious is programmed to think from the present time, *backward*. It will search through many layers of experiences until it finds the core belief of a problem. It will use this belief, which is usually from past memory, to create present day action. Seldom is the answer from our present situation. Consciously --which is the present time -- you are unaware of how you are thinking or reacting from this past belief information.

"The core of the memory may be negative, but a memory lived as real is called a perception. The quest to understand why we do what we do is because, unless the core issue or core belief is found and dealt with, the relief of understanding will be short.

"To create permanent change and enjoy permanent relief, the very depth or core information must be found, worked with and understood. This, when integrated, will give a flood of relief with permanent, positive change.

"Illya," he repeated to them, "do this and your pain and confusion will balance into understanding. I will repeat:

- Identify the negative feeling.
- Tap one tap on the Forehead, then one tap on the Thymus with the right hand.
- Move the right hand over your heart and hold for a few seconds to remove collected information.
- With the right hand on the heart, *now reprogram.*
- Say positive affirmations by starting with, I AM..., I DO..., I CHOOSE...."

The light in the room faded to normal, and Illya and her father were alone. Their bodies continued to glow from the effects of the Light. They looked iridescent.

At last, Illya broke the silence. "Father, did you see him and hear him? I feel that we have received a way to release the turmoil, doubt, and confusion that has been plaguing my mind from watching Derth die."

"Yes, Illya, we both saw and heard. We must do what the Light Being has taught us to do. This will help me release grief from the loss of Enya. Illya, you do the tapping, and let's see what happens."

Illya identified these emotions: "I am worried, sad, confused and troubled about Derth's death." She tapped with her right hand on her forehead and then one tap on her thymus. Then, she put that same hand over her heart. She held it there for a few seconds before saying, "I am peaceful. I am energized. I choose balance. I do trust that God loves me, and He alone is in charge of me."

When she was finished, Illya felt relief and a surge of energy. She knew all the changes were complete. Her mind cleared, the confusion left, and she felt wonderful. "Father," she said, "this works. I feel balanced, rational, and whole for the first time in days."

Father said, "This is very important. We will teach this Gift to our kingdom."

Illya retired to her room, completed nightly preparations, and climbed into bed. Then, she prayed and poured out her heart in thankfulness for all that she had received. She began to breathe deeply and allowed herself to drift into a meditative state as her father had taught her. "This is a wonderful feeling," she thought.

Just then, she felt a presence. "Oh, no," she thought, "He's back!" She pulled the pillow over her head. "I just can't do any more of this!"

It was Derth! She knew his energy! No one had his same energy! He was in her room! It seemed as though he was saying something. She lifted one side of the pillow. "What was he saying?" This time she wasn't telepathically connected. She was trying to physically hear him, but it was not working.

Derth seemed to know this and finally got through to her. "Go tell my wife. Go give her and my children the integration! *Please, please,* go tell my wife!"

Illya jumped out of bed, put on a robe, and went to find her father. "Father, Father, Derth has been here. He told me that he wants us to go to his wife and children. He wants their grief and loss lifted from them. He wants me to tell his wife that I have seen him. He wants us to give them the integration, and he wants them to know that he is happy and alive in spirit."

The next day the horses were hitched to the carriage, and the King and Illya went immediately to Derth's family where they were warmly received. Illya told Derth's wife she had seen him after his death and he was happy and alive in Spirit. The King and Illya began teaching the integration to Derth's wife and children. Immediately, new energy came into the family. Illya smiled. She noticed the five-year-old boy integrate the new little baby. This family had instantly changed and now had happy smiles as they waved good-bye to their friends, the King and Illya.

CB

Back at the castle, classes began first with those who worked or lived at the castle. On the second day of instruction, Parel brought clean linens to the castle. She accepted the invitation to take part in the class. She willingly went through the steps and received the information. She felt released, balanced, and happy.

Parel fell to her knees, "May I help teach the Gift of Integration?" she asked. The King raised her from her knees and told her to thank God, not him. Because of her honest behavior, she deserved to have this reward.

He said she could work with Him and Illya, and they began the training to teach the people in the Kingdom immediately.

☙

A year passed and Parel was in close contact, working with the King and Illya. All those who were working with the Light, teaching honesty and prayer, and feeling the joy of how it all fit with the 'Gift', had drawn very close to one another. The feelings of love and devotion were strong. Parel still took care of the linens in the castle. Washing and ironing were easy for her to do. She could not do enough to show her gratitude for the Gift and for Illya and the King, for he had saved her life more than once.

As Parel was teaching a class about honesty, the King was listening as she spoke. His mind reflected back to the Parel of a year ago. Through the love of God and the integration, a multitude of positive changes had taken place. He thought, "Not just to Parel but also to the entire Kingdom."

Parel and Father

The King looked at Parel as though he was seeing her for the first time. She pleased the male eye as she was beautiful in a strong clean way.

Parel was a little taller than most women. This gave her a stately look. She was viewed as elegant in self-made, hand-tailored robes. She had many beautiful skills and one of them was the care she gave her hair.

Her dark hair curled naturally as it tumbled over her shoulders and down her back. It looked abundant, shiny, and alive. Her complexion was clear with rosy cheeks. Her eyes were dark but changed as she spoke into a smoky purple hue. "Very unusual," he thought. He could imagine a golden crown nestled in her hair as she wore a queen's robe of purple velvet to match those eyes.

The King flushed, feeling embarrassed, and he turned his head so she would not notice he had been watching her.

"I wonder," he thought. "What if she moved to a cottage on the palace grounds? There would be plenty of space for her and the children. I'll tell the servants to prepare one of the cottages. Illya loves Parel. She will be happy with this decision. The castle has been so lonely since Enya died and left us for the Great Beyond. It will be nice to hear children playing again. Yes, this is good. She has boys the same age as Aka. Playmates. Illya would have Parel's womanly ways to feel close to. And I," he mused, "will have a friend to continue teaching the integration with."

❧

As Illya's hands rested upon the windowsill of the tower, she shivered as the cool evening breeze reminded her that it was time to go down the winding stairs and into the castle.

She said in a motherly tone, "Come, Aka. It's time to go down to bed."

She thought, "I am now eighteen years old. It has been almost a month since Father and Parel married. It has been two years since the visitation of the Light Being. Father and I have been teaching and instructing the entire kingdom on how to become and remain positive and in the Light of God by using the integration. It has taken two years of hard work, but Father, Parel, Aka and I, finally completed this goal. The integration teaches how to use the body and mind to remove negative thoughts and replace them with good ones. I am thankful to my God for this Gift and all those who helped teach me.

"When you teach a truth concept, negative thoughts will change in one person. Thus the propensity to change the whole world, one person at a time.

"God's love and Light are positive. This is what we wanted for our Kingdom. We wanted our people to know God and make their own changes to become positive. We wanted all to grow in God's Light."

She patted Aka on the back. "Now, you and I go wherever we want in our kingdom, and we are safe. There was Father, Parel and you (She poked Aka in a teasing way.) and me." (She pointed to herself playfully.) With a big smile on her face, "We have done this together. (She hugged her brother.)

"With God, anything and everything is possible, Aka."

God's light and love was in every heart. This made everyone safe. All the corruption had ceased. Every person in the kingdom loved God. This made obedience and truth the laws of the land. Father no longer had to spend excess time in court.

Those who did not like what was being taught moved to another village, taking their evil ways with them. With their dark energy gone, the Light in the Kingdom was now very close to the same Light that was with the Light being who brought the Integration. *As each day passed, the clearness of this beautiful Light increased. This is what everyone in the kingdom wanted, more and more of God's Light and Love.*

PART TWO
NOW

Courtney and Jennifer

T he class bell rang. Courtney stacked her books in her backpack and headed to the school parking lot to find her car, then go home. Every day she parked in a different spot, thus finding her car was always a bit of a challenge. The fee for a permanent parking spot was more than she wanted to pay. She would rather give extra money for her car payment.

"There it is." She breathed a sigh of relief. It was closer then she remembered. She threw her books in the back seat, plopped into the driver seat, and fished in her pocket for the keys. When would she ever remember to put her keys in her hand before she sat down in the car and shut the door?

High school graduation was one week away. She had mixed feelings about it. She was glad high school was almost finished, but it meant many changes would take place in her life. The prospects of college were exciting, and the eagerness of going away to school made her happy, yet sad.

With that thought, apprehension set in. She sat for a moment thinking about her job at Dillard's for the summer, then she would be gone.

Now her racing mind skipped to her parents and the safety she would be leaving behind. Would it ever be the same again? Sadness crept in as she thought about leaving her friends and family. All her friends were going to different schools. Would she ever connect with them again? Her heart swelled with hope as she anticipated:

"Old friends are golden, new friends are silver, but can become golden with time." They will always be my friends. I will make new ones at college but will love keeping in touch with my dear, golden friends.

Yesterday, Courtney had almost fallen down the stairs at school. As her mind re-played the experience, she grimaced. She had missed a step on the second floor stairs and went into a free fall, landing on top of a kid named Barry who just happened to be coming up the stairs at the very moment she fell. Luckily, he had caught her in his arms! Ugh!

She was grateful he had been there, but she remembered how he had held her longer than necessary. How embarrassing!

She had a sinking feeling as she wondered how many had seen him keep his arms around her and squeeze her to him. She had squirmed in resistance but he just squeezed tighter. She realized every move she made was making him feel her body more and made it worse!

Thinking about it again made her cringe and her face feel hot all over again. She looked into her deep brown eyes in her visor mirror. Her brown hair framed the red flush that began in her neck. She put her hands over her cheeks as she remembered feeling his body in contact with hers, all *the way down as she squirmed!*

Finally, she stopped. Then she wedged her arms between them and pushed hard against his chest. His sour breath spread over her face and into her nostrils.

He was a head taller and seventy five pounds heavier than her five foot four inch slender frame. He immediately released his hold. She could have died a thousand deaths!

When she thanked him for catching her, he puffed his foul breath into her face and said with a smile that was too sweet, "My pleasure!" Then he attempted to squeeze her again.

Her mind recoiled and she screamed, "Oh, No!" and her stomach revolted as she got free of him.

Here in her car she was safe, but her face flamed bright red all over again. She felt sick and violated. It would have been so much better if he had only helped her not hugged her!

Throughout school, they were in many of the same classes. At times there would be a feeling that someone was looking at her and it was always Barry! He wanted *to sit* near her; and come to think of it, he had always violated her space. She avoided him all the time until that accident on the stairs. She cringed again. "He is definitely not my style!" she exclaimed to herself. He was always dressed in weird clothing and wore strange earrings. His friends were different. Some of them wore nose rings and had tattoos all over their bodies. Most of them had at least one arm covered from wrist to shoulder with symbols of girls and sometimes even across the shoulders.

She simply preferred people who were clean-cut and looked like they had just stepped from a fresh shower. Most young women at eighteen were starting to look for suitable young men to keep company with and getting to know well enough to consider marriage, eventually. They didn't have to be perfect in their dress, just clean; and they had to get decent grades in school and have life goals. Courtney did not want friends who made weak choices. Nor did she want to be tempted to live a life different from how she had grown up. She did not approve of Hollywood's depiction of life in television and in movies. She wanted to live her life as close to the Light of God as possible.

Courtney could remember a time when Barry had been quite decent but slowly had changed to what he was now. He had chosen to go with the wrong crowd. This was just more evidence that people slowly become like the people with whom they keep company. She wanted to be very careful with whom she spent her time. She was better off alone than compromise her values to be with just anyone. The old saying that one rotten apple spoils the whole barrelful was definitely true.

Being like everyone else was never what Courtney wanted. She knew who she was and had never rebelled against goodness because she loved her parents and her life full of love and Jesus. She came into the world with that love; and her parents, who also love Jesus, reinforced it. She understood how to have the Spirit in her life and use it.

Having received many answers to her prayers, she knew those true feelings when the Spirit whispered to her Soul. When this happened, she always got goose bumps and felt chills. It started at the back of her head and descended down her spine, with her chest on fire. Yet she felt peaceful, all at the same time. Then her thoughts cleared with understanding. When this whisper took place, confusion dropped away. She now knew strongly who she was and what she needed to do. She had received one of these answers about which college she should attend in the fall.

Then her mind shifted to thinking about leaving for UCLA. She became very conscious of the things her mother did for her. She now reflected on them and wondered what she would do without her mother. Then this hopeful thought came: "Thank goodness for unlimited minutes on cell phones! My Mother is my best friend. I will need to talk to her often."

Her mind shifted to other things that concerned her. Her mother helped her in mega ways, but lately especially, with her thoughts. Mother always told her, "**Positive in, Negative out**." She had learned that to be positive was very important in a negative world. Her mother always corrected her negative words with positive statements that Courtney collected and repeated often as positive affirmations. However, the same negative problems did come back more often than she wanted. Affirmations did not work well all the time; or if they did, it was very slow. Why was there no easy, positive way to stay strong and make the changes one wanted to make in life?

She thought, "It would be wonderful if people were like a computer and had a button to push to change all their negative programs to positive.

Push the button and empty all the garbage just like a recycle bin on a computer."

Courtney now thought about her eighteenth birthday, when her parents had literally released her to freedom. They told her she would have no parental supervision unless she asked for it. She was free to make her own decisions. Her parents deeply loved her. A gift of that love was not only being an example but also of two happy people and how they had worked together in raising and caring for her!

She thought about how her parents had carefully screened all media coming into their home: music, the seldom used television, and movies that were G rated. There was a time she wanted to be like everyone else, but eventually she realized the commitment her parents had made to each other and her so they would have a positive environment for Courtney.

They were *selfless* and had taken great care in what they watched so she would value clean, uplifting entertainment.

Her word and truth were united. She knew this was the most important asset she could have. **Others knew she spoke the truth and kept her word**. She wanted to continue doing that. She wanted those she kept company with to do the same. Courtney knew she had excellent parents. Truth had been the family's way of life. It was what they were.

She was now considered an adult. This meant her parents wanted her to make her own decisions from now on. They said they would council her and help her in any way, but they would be a friend, not instructor. She was grateful she could be who she was and that her parents were giving her deep unconditional love.

Now her mind skipped to her car. She had accepted debt two years ago when she purchased it. Having a car paid for would be a great advantage, and she had two payments left. She could hardly wait for the last one to be over. She would drive her car to UCLA free of debt.

Courtney had taken good care of her red Nissan and loved having a clean and shiny car. She named her car "Pet". The movie Aladdin was popular at the time she got her car. Aladdin rode or flew around on a red carpet. Since she rode around in a red car, she called it her Car- Pet which evolved into "Pet". When she first started using the term "Pet" for her car, her friends thought she had a dog. Well, she was taking her Pet to school with her, but it certainly was not a dog!

Courtney backed out of the parking space, shifted into gear, and pulled into the street. She glanced into her rear view mirror, checking for traffic. She then looked ahead down her lane. With horror, she saw a black car coming straight at her. Her foot automatically went to her brakes, but it was too late. The oncoming car crashed into her head on. It hit her with a crunching, smashing, head-on force that pushed her bright red 'Pet', smashed and broken, to the side of the road in a whirling, smoky, broken mass.

Courtney was knocked unconscious and did not know what had happened to her or her beautiful, almost paid for, car.

❧

Jennifer was driving too fast. The black BMW was new. It had a V-8 engine, so it was powerful. It had been a gift from her husband, Keith, for their thirty-second wedding anniversary. Jennifer reflected on her marriage to Keith. They shared a good life. He loved her and appreciated her; most importantly, he always did little things for her to show his love. She loved this kind and rare type of husband and felt very fortunate and blessed that Keith had been by her side through thick and thin these many years. One of their greatest joys was the time they spent with family, traveling and doing family things together like going to church, camping and meeting at the park for picnics and softball. This relationship with her family made her very happy.

She and Keith were parents of two children, now adults. She absentmindedly reflected on her children and their lives as she drove, too fast, down the street.

Their oldest child, a daughter Annie, was a joy and doing well. She had married Tom Hill, a very nice young man just over a year ago. They had recently brought Jennifer's first grandchild into the world.

Shawn was a cute, chubby, little boy with a head full of black curly hair. There were special feelings about this first grandchild. Jennifer's joy was complete in this little boy. When looking for family features, she found her father's toes repeated one more time.

Their nineteen-year-old son, David, was trying to grow-up too fast and not making good choices. David continually teased Tom and Annie of being over the Hill as this was their name. Now they had another Hill by the name of Shawn. How many Hills were they going to bring into the world to go over the hill? She chuckled to herself. David could be very funny at times, but this was not one of those times.

He was the reason she was hurrying. He was in college at UCLA. It was his first year. Jennifer had received a telephone call at work informing her that David had been arrested and was in jail. The officer told her that drugs were involved. Her mind agonized, "How can this be? When your children are infants and close around your knee, you feel they would always be safe from the drug world. It would never touch your children. It can't be David! It just isn't possible. How does a child change so much? This has to be a mistake! Her David would never do this. He has always been the kindest, sweetest little boy. How can this happen?"

He had had a lot of experience making incorrect decisions. He started making them in his junior year in high school. She had talked to him about bringing honor to himself, not disgrace. He was keeping company with the wrong crowd. David had brought her much heartache and stress this year. At first, she thought he was just sowing a few wild oats and would soon get a grip, becoming the person she knew he could be.

Jennifer's mind began to rationalize. She was not paying enough attention to her driving. This was his first year away from home and was living in a dormitory. With this arrest, he would have to find some other place to live. The University would no longer allow him to live in the dorm. Perhaps he would have to move back home. "This would be good," she reasoned. "He needs to grow up a little more."

Her mind began wondering why David had put his values aside and made these decisions even though he knew better. Two children born and raised in the same pod, turned out so different. How could his sister be truthful and balanced, while he was such a challenge? What had she done wrong? Was it her fault?

She was driving too fast, because in her mind, she was on fast forward to get to the police station and David.

Jennifer's cell phone began to play *her call sound*. Perhaps it was David. She reached to get the phone, but it was not in the usual place. "Where was it?" She searched with her right hand and could not find it, all the while watching the road but with no results. She looked down, "The phone must have fallen to the floor. There it is!" she said. It rang again! She stretched as far as she could to retrieve it. She could feel it with the tip of her fingers. Just a little farther! She took her eyes off of the road, glanced down, put her hand on the phone and quickly looked up. In a nano-second she had drifted across the middle line. She was paralyzed with shock! There was a red car directly in her path! She applied the brakes, but it was too late.

☙

Three days later, Courtney woke up in the hospital. The pain in her head and body was unbearable. She struggled to open her eyes.

"Oh, good. You are finally awake," the nurse explained. "You have a concussion." Then she gave Courtney an injection for pain. Courtney vaguely heard the nurse mention room 319. She thought, "Is room 319 where I am? What am I doing here? It feels so-o-o good to be out of pain and drifting." Instantly, she was asleep again.

☙

Jennifer never lost consciousness. She had relived the accident many times in the last three days. Would she ever go to sleep again without the car wreck flashing through her mind? When she crashed into the red car, she was thrown into the dash tearing her lower jaw. Then she jetted into the ceiling where she sustained head and spinal injuries. But she was not as badly hurt as the woman in the red car, who was taken away in an ambulance.

She remembered, as she drifted half asleep, that two men in white had held her at the ceiling of the car as it spun out of control. They had asked her, "Do you want to live?"

Instantly, the thought of her husband, children, and grandchild flashed through her mind. "I do want to live! I do want to be there for my family and my grandchild. Please give me more time to live!" The two men in white let her drop into the seat just as her car was completing the spin that twisted her and turned her with intense, snapping force. Her muscles were stretched beyond normal limit. Her back and joints were forced out of their sockets, somehow without ever breaking. She felt pain as she had never felt it before.

She had been mostly conscious the past three days because she could not sleep. Only pain pills sedated her enough to let her sleep for short intervals. The pain had come in waves, excruciating and blinding pain that sent her to the floor if not supported. She wore a neck brace and a back support. It was an elastic wrap with bonelike stays in it, which helped immensely. Physical therapy helped bring blood supply and shape back into her injured muscles. As she thought about the two men in white and the question they had asked her, she realized that **Some people are given a choice between life and death this decision is made continually.**

Jennifer had a lot of time to think. She had already found the pain could be removed through prayer and calling upon the *Light of God by* envisioning God and His Son Jesus in a circle of Light, sending a column of light to her head in the form of a conduit going straight down through her. The Light was then in her, around her, and penetrating completely through her. She practiced keeping the Light with her; because when she had this Light, she felt peaceful with lessened pain. Because of this, she tried very hard to keep this as her state of mind.

❧

Courtney was doing somewhat better with no shots for pain but pain pills every four hours. The nurses insisted she get out of bed and walk a few steps. That was very hard! Her head felt as though a huge truck had run over it. It felt impossible to hold her head up without a bulky neck brace. She could not believe she had been asleep for three days. "All I remember is a black car coming at me," she thought. "I remember nothing else." She looked across the hall and saw the room 319. Courtney recalled that was the number mentioned by the nurses, and she wondered who was in that room.

෪

On the fourth day, Jennifer felt improved. She got out of bed, reached stiffly for a robe, then slowly headed into the hallway. If she could only walk the length of the hallway, the nurse had said she would be ready to go home. In the hall she passed a woman with her head in bandages and a large brace around her neck. She appeared to be young. The hospital robe engulfed her small shape. Perhaps she was a teenager, but she was no more than twenty. She had a lovely face and dark eyes. "I wonder what color her hair is," she thought.

A nurse supported the young woman on each side as she struggled to take a few steps. The nurses patiently encouraged her to place one foot in front of the other.

Shortly after Jennifer returned to her room, one of the nurses also came to help her. Jennifer asked, "Who was the young woman in the hall?"

"You both came in at the same time. I think you were in the same car accident." A mental image flashed into Jennifer's mind of a brown haired woman being carried to an ambulance. She immediately sensed that the white bandages covered brown hair. The nurse informed her that the young woman's name was Courtney.

Jennifer was in distress about causing the accident. She often wished she could turn the clock back. How she wished she had ignored her cell phone that afternoon. She felt a strong desire to talk Courtney. " I must ask her for forgiveness as soon as possible," she thought. "I want to tell her how awful I feel for being responsible for the accident. I now know through a hard experience that **Cell phones and driving do not mix.**

"As soon as I can walk the hallway by myself, I will talk to her."

ɞ

Courtney closed her eyes. The pain pill was working. "I hurt so bad! Never in my life have I been in such pain! I do not want this intense pain. Instead I want to drift and float, the pill has made me so relaxed." Her eyes started to close, but sensed a presence next to her bed. She jerked awake. There stood a rather tall woman in her late forties who she recognized as the woman coming out of room 319.

Large dark bruises covered the woman's face and arms. They were especially bad around her eyes. Although the bruises were very prominent, one could see past this that she was a beautiful woman, a very nice, kind, gentle soul. Even with blackened eyes, she had poise. Courtney felt she was a kindred spirit to this woman. Who was she?

Then Jennifer spoke with much empathy. Her voice was soft and cultured. "I understand you and I had an accident. I am so sorry you were hurt." Her eyes filled with tears, "I care so much. Can you ever forgive me?"

ᥐ

Many chance meetings at various appointments with doctors or at physical therapy had brought Courtney and Jennifer together often. They talked very easily with one another. Ideas passed back and forth on various subjects, and their minds were the same on most topics. It was amazing how much alike they were. If Jennifer was younger or Courtney older, they would be doing many of the same things at the same time. They became close friends quickly in spite of the age difference.

They exchanged phone numbers and agreed they would never use the phone while driving. Talk was endless about pain and releasing pain. They learned that acupuncture and physical therapy helped to release some of the pain for a short time. Most modalities for healing helped, but did not completely remove the pain. In fact, the pain often returned with a vengeance. Courtney's healing was still in a very painful stage. She often had headaches. She found that cranial therapy with emotional release helped more than anything. It relieved most of the pain for longer periods of time.

One day Courtney went to Jennifer's home to visit. Courtney dropped into the corner chair saying. "You know, Jen, it would be wonderful if there was some way that God could touch us and stop our pain, healing our tendons and muscles. I have always felt *we are like computers.* If so, 'Please God, give me a *button* to push on my personal computer. I want to get rid of all this pain and put it in the garbage can.'" Then Courtney laughed. "We have so much pain, I can see red buttons plastered all over us saying, 'Push me. Push me.' Let's face it, we need a miracle!"

"Sure, Courtney, but there are other types of pain. What about grief, aloneness, separation, and loss.? I wish God would touch me so that I could help everyone. There is so much pain in the world. There is a need to release physical, emotional, mental pain. What about addictions? This is pain! My son has extreme pain; his pain in turn causes me more pain. We need God to bless us with a great big red button...I wonder, would this free us?"

"Jennifer, perhaps we could ask God if this is possible. Since we are like computers and if there is a key, a special key, that allowes all negative to leave our bodies, minds, and feelings, it would be an exceptional gift."

No sooner did they speak these words than an amazing, shimmering, crystal clear, W*hite Light appeared in the room*. There were two beings in this beautiful light, a male and a female. A beautiful feeling of love filled the room engulfing them in complete silence and wonder.

The iridescent male spoke, calling them by name. "Jennifer and Courtney, we have come to help you."

Both women had a deep peaceful feeling, realizing that these two beings had been sent by God.

"We have been sent to give you a Gift. This gift left the earth about 2500 BC. My daughter, Illya, and I lived on the earth at that time. We and our whole kingdom used this Gift from God to lift us to a higher, stronger, clearer dimension of Light. We all live there now. Our main purpose is to serve God and help others wanting clearness with God.

"It was a wicked time for our earth. However, we who had the Gift became so filled with the Light of God that it became our nature. We were taken off the earth and lifted up into heaven, not by death, but by *transformation.* Everyone in our kingdom accepted this Gift and used it only with prayer. We live in a different dimension of energy than you do. There is no death where we are. We serve *God the Father* and assist *His Son Jesus Christ* as messengers, working with *His Holy Angels.*"

The young woman, Illya, was dressed in a gown of sparkling material that shimmered with every movement. "My name is Illya," she said. "We have heard your plea. God sent us to give you our G*ift.* My father and I taught the people in our kingdom to release negative thinking, pain, and grief from the mind, feelings, and body. When this is done, you become whole in body and spirit. The negative emotional memory of the past is gone.

"This *is* what you have asked for. It is not exactly a big red button, as you suggested, but it **is** on the body. It is what we lovingly refer to as the *'Gift'!* It will release your negative thoughts, pain, grief and depression. It works the same as one of your modern day computers that releases garbage from its hard drive at the press of a button."

As the man stepped forward, his luminous aura moved with him. His light was so wondrously beautiful that the colors of the rainbow were around him, changing from *golden light to a shimmering White Light, more brilliant than the sun.*

"*I am King Enoch.* I am a prophet of God and I governed a kingdom upon this earth many years ago. At one time, there was much wickedness in the land. I asked *God* to help me find a way to stop the wickedness, and He blessed me by giving me the *Gift* as an answer to my prayer. *The Gift opens a door to the Light, love, and energy of God. If you have not been able to pray, you will be able to after using the Gift. When you give all your troubles to God and use this gift, it will empower you to clear all your energy to become Light.*

"It will erase susceptibility to illness, and your body will go through a physical and emotional cleanse. This allows stressed areas to relax. As you relax, it releases poisons so a purifying cleanse of the body can begin. During this cleanse, you will want to drink quarts, even a gallon, of purified water daily. As all your energy clears to the Light, you will go through many cleanses. All of the cleanses will register in the physical but will also be emotional and mental. Negative emotions will be changed into acceptance, balance, peace, and unconditional love."

The King went on to explain, "This wondrous gift is the *Gift of Integration*. Integration balances all the areas of the physical body. The physical body is more than just physical matter. It has twelve energy centers, or chakras. Each chakra has Infinite energy levels within it. They are as follows:

LOCATION	GOVERNS
1. Pelvis	Fight or flight, grounding to earth and family
2. Navel	Self-nurturing or nurturing of others
3. Solar Plexus	Personal power, supporting yourself and others
4. Heart	Love, self, others, receiving, giving
5. Throat	Decisions, choosing the Light of God
6. Forehead	Third eye, intuition, abundance and self-reality
7. Crown	Connection to spirituality and God
8. Back of head	Joy and fulfillment
9. Back of throat	Charity the pure love of God
10. Back of heart	Hope as a future with God
11. Back of solar plexus	Faith, blindly knowing there is a God
12. Lumbar and sacrum meet	Eternal progression, and your first creation

"All twelve centers, when grounded to God's love and Light, will balance all energy in the physical body as peace.

"Twelve is a Celestial number," the King explained. "There are other twelve's that are significant to the human body. They are automatically included in the first twelve energy centers. They are:

- twelve expanded colors in the chakras.
- twelve acupuncture meridians.
- twelve cranial nerves.
- twelve tissue salts.
- twelve organ systems.
- twelve disciples/apostles.
- twelve tribes.
- twelve gemstones.
- twelve tones on the music scale.
- Twelve levels in each energy center.

"Twelve is truly a Celestial number," said the King.

He continued, "From our first existence to the present time, we have moved through numerous stages of progression. Thus, you have been in transition for eons. You were first Intelligence as matter *Unorganized.* Then, your choice was to be intelligent matter O*rganized.* This, then, became *our Individual Intelligence.* You next become a S*pirit Child of God where you could become as*

God our Father, Who gave us our spirit body and life plan.

"There is a permanent record of your existence held in the master cell of your forehead area. It is still recording everything that happens to you. It always has and it always will.

"Becoming human is very special. *'For as man is; God once was. As God is, man may become.'*

"We have inherited God's perfection in our perfect spirit. Therefore, because we have chosen to become as God is, we are on this physical earth to do just that.

"Humans have a brain cortex different from any other living thing. Most animals have only an upper cortex. Humans have an upper and lower cortex. This gives us the ability to know right from wrong. This allows us to become like our God. Thus, we have a perfect blueprint because our brain is shaped and formed with the same configuration as God's brain.

"This means that as an organized intelligence, we chose to be a God or Goddess creator with **divine *attributes of truth***. We then received a spirit body, which remembers being with God. It also remembers the existence of perfect love and peace we had when we lived with Him. We long to go back, but we cannot. ***Ours is not a path of regression but of going forward, continually progressing.*** However, through understanding and obeying God's Ten Commandments and loving Him as our Father and Jesus Christ as our brother, who is also the God of this world, can live with Him on this earth in a Godlike state.

"You chose your family pod in the pre-existent state. After you steadily progressed to the point of being ready to become created physically, conception happened. In a nano-second, all components of your creation came together; and your physical body was formed. This became the home for your spirit body. At some point in time between conception and birth, if not at birth, the spirit body came into the physical body. It gives the body life and energy. Up to that time, you existed on your earth Mother's energy.

"The physical body is made up of trillions of cells. They come from both sides of your family and are called progenitor cells. At the time of conception, the cellular collection of all the cells that make up your body is automatically done. These body-building cells are called DNA and RNA. They swirl and blend, creating genetics that form the body which your spirit will enter and live in while alive on this earth.

"This makes massive subconscious programs that will govern ninety-nine percent of all our daily thoughts and actions. All of this creative energy is locked in the subconscious part of your mind and is basically unknown. But the subconscious becomes the director of what we are and what we do every day of our life. If we were to compare the size of the sub-conscious to a physical size, the base would be as big as one of your city blocks and as tall as a ten-story skyscraper. The conscious part of us acts out the subconscious but is only the size of a small box sitting on top of the skyscraper.

"In your mortal state, the hardest and immense task to conquer is learning to govern the conscious mind.

"This is why I have brought you the Gift. With the gift you will be able to progress to your ultimate self, which is to bring the intelligence, spirit and physical body together with God's energy and Light."

The Integration

King Enoch continued his instruction. "You are now ready to use the G*ift* I am giving you. It is called, '*Integration'*.

"The Integration is a protected, collective pool of knowledge. When used with God's Love, it neutralizes negative emotion. Then God's Light, Love and peace flood in, making your life in balance.

"It is a gift from God. With His love, it completes enough power to heal and clear most emotional, mental, physical, and/or spiritual problems. The *Integration* releases all negative patterning and programs that keep you from becoming the ultimate you, who *always wants perfect Light, love, and health.*

"This *Gift of Integration will only be effective* when you *first pray. Prayer clears your space and* connects you to the Light. You then think or visualize the Light coming to you as a column or beam of Light from God, our Eternal Father.

"You may want to say a prayer such as, 'God, the Eternal Father, in the name of Jesus Christ of Nazareth, who died for me and lives for me and through the Holy Spirit, please connect me to your Light.'

"The Light from God will come to you, go through you, be around you, and in you, all at the same moment. It is given like a laser beam. For all of its power, pray and ask for it to come. It is called, 'White Light.' It is total peace, love, balance, and harmony. White Light is our God connection and is what we are searching for all of our life. When we are in the Light, we are peaceful and happy.

"*This is **using Clear-ology to clear your space**! As human beings, we have been given a gift to heal ourselves. (Luke 4:23, Physician, heal thyself.)* This allows us to become clear so we can heal ourself.

"We are two sided," said the King. "Our brains are genetically formed with a right hemisphere, giving us emotion and feelings, and a left hemisphere, giving us analytical, logical qualities. When these two hemispheres are out of balance, there is chaos. The integration deletes the negative differences and creates a whole, balanced brain, being filled with His love.

"Here is *the process of Integration:*

118

"Tap with your right hand on your forehead over the Master cell, Pineal or Third eye. Then tap on the upper chest below the notch in your nec, on the area of the Thymus. Then bring your right hand over your heart. This deletes the negative information; and our body, much like a computer, can now receive new information.

"With your right hand resting over your heart, now by word or thought word, it must be filled back up again. Think 'The Light' and then say positive affirmations. This seals the emptied space with Light.

"An affirmation is declaring a truth that is positive and filled with Light and goodwill. When declared, it now becomes the program to live by."

The King went into specific details, explaining how Courtney and Jennifer could remove their pain. The steps are outlined here:

- Clear your space through prayer.
- Identify the problem. Feel it to the *greatest degree* you have ever felt it.
- *Tap* on the forehead with the *right hand*, then the *thymus.* (This says to the body, "Computer, collect all the negative in all of my energy and creation.")

- Move your *right hand* to your *heart.* (This is the *elimination button,* or in your personal computer, the garbage can.) Hold for a few seconds.
- Put the same *hand* over your *heart.* (You've now made an empty hole in your programming which needs to be filled with positive input.)
- Say, "**I choose** to be comfortable in my body. **I do** love my body. **I am** releasing my body to balance, to be comfortable and pain free."

Courtney did as she was instructed. It was amazing! She felt the pain lift from her head. It was gone! "Thank you, God. Thank you." she exclaimed..

"Jennifer," said the King, "You have much grief and pain in your heart. You have a son on drugs. This causes you to feel intense pain. This pain has manifested itself in your spine. Let us clear it from your body.

"Clear your space. Connect to the Light of God. *Identify your pain. Feel* it in your heart and also in your spine. Identify grief, fear, suffering, and loss.

"*Tap on the* forehead and *thymus.* There were other times in your life and existence when you experienced these same feelings.

They are now being magnified in the present experience. Tapping on the forehead will collect it from all your past energy, to infinity and forever. Tap your right hand on your Thymus and hold. This will erase it.

"*Move the right hand to your heart*. Re-program saying, "*I choose* to allow my son his life experience. *I am* releasing him now to his pathway. *I am* free of his pain. *I am free* to love. I choose David and love. *I am tough love; I do* give my love but stay strong. *I am* releasing the burden of emotional weight from my back."

After Jennifer went through the steps, she exclaimed, "I feel the changes. The pain is lifting. The pain is now gone! Thank you, God! Thank you! Thank you!"

"Remember," said Illya. "Anything can be changed, but it will only work in the *presence of prayer* and the *Light of God the Eternal Father* and the *Holy Spirit*."

"Remember, this is the order," the King reminded.

- Pray and clear your space to God.
- Identify the negative feeling. Then intensify it to the greatest degree you have ever felt it.

- Tap with the right hand on the forehead, then thymus.
- Then put that same hand over your heart.
- With your right hand over the heart, reprogram with positive affirmations. Start with, I CHOOSE..., I DO..., I AM...."

The light in the room began to fade. Jennifer and Courtney had no idea how long they had been with these beautiful Light Beings. But in their hearts, they knew the significance of what they had been given.

They began immediately to clear one another, using the integration to bring a new level of love of God, goodness, and joy in life.

☙

SIX MONTHS LATER

Courtney and Jennifer continued processing with the Integration. Many negative programs were being brought forth and examined. They were carefully doing as the King had told them to do. They had been integrating on loving themselves, allowing themselves to be loved, giving love, receiving and accepting God's love, as well as affirming, "I am loveable."

Courtney said, "When I was in high school, my parents suggested I use positive affirmations, but I gave up. I had done hundreds of them and needed to do hundreds more. They didn't work. However, now with the integration, I feel them enter my heart. It's as though the affirmation is already who I am."

AFFIRM YOUR SELF TO BE AN OPTIMIST!

By prayer say, *"Father in Heaven, I love you. Through the Atonement of Jesus Christ, please forgive me. I am sorry. I forgive (the offender). Thank you! I release (this) to you, Father, and ask it to be deleted from my programming Now and throughout Infinity and Forever!"* As you say this place your right hand over your forehead. Then thymus, then heart, repeating these positive affirmations. (write your own affirmations in between).

- *God, the Universe and I are one in "Light" energy.*
- *God is first, then my Mate, Me, my Family, Work and Friends. This is the order of peace.*
- *I am passionate about truth, always keeping time commitments and setting honest boundaries.*
- *I am healthy, strong and capable. Every growing experience in life brings knowledge and peace.*
- *I am moving forward with confidence and joy. All is well in my life and future.*
- *I am speaking health, happiness, prosperity, and abundance to everyone I know.*

- *I am abundantly prosperous in all ways. I share my wealth with others less fortunate.*
- *I am assuring to my friends, giving truth and wisdom. I make them feel special.*
- *I am an excellent self-starter, the sunny side of everything. I make optimism come true.*
- *I am expecting only the best. My work and work place are the best.*
- *I am feeling Divine guidance with success and gratitude for myself and others.*
- *I am releasing all pain, in, on, or between my emotional, mental, spiritual bodies, past, present and future. Pain is GONE, NOW!*
- *I am cheerful, smiling at every person in my life and in my relationships.*
- *I honor the excellence of love in myself and look for it in others.*
- *I am noble, fearless, happy and thankful. Goodwill flows from me, to me, from every source.*
- *I am personally wealthy in my finances and business Prosperity is mine, NOW!*
- *I am alive to enjoy exploring all things of who "I AM".*

"I yearn to give the Integration to my sister." Jennifer said. "She has a lot of negative in her life and wants to be more positive. I would love to let this bless her life. I just do not know when that will happen. She lives in Canada, and I only see her once a year."

Again, the room began filling with Light. It was the same beautiful, shimmering light containing all the colors of the rainbow going from gold to crystal clear to White Light. The King was there again in the Light. He had returned to give them more information.

He said, "I am here to answer your questions about how to help your sister in Canada know about prayer and muscle testing, and show you how negative DNA programming can be changed to positive.

⊂ℨ

D. N. A.

"To enable understanding of the full process, I will explain the principles of genetics," the King continued. "Our body cells are made up of a nucleus, which contains threadlike particles called chromosomes. A  chromosome is formed from a single DNA (Deoxyribonucleic Acid) molecule that contains many genes. The DNA molecule is a long, spiraling double strand or helix. Chromosomes connect the strands like rungs on a ladder. DNA is the material that holds the codes for the many physical characteristics of every living creature. Cells use different codes to determine what functions to carry out, just as language is used to communicate. All the directions for the structure and functioning of the body is contained in the chromosomes through DNA.

"During the first twelve days of the development of the embryo, a spiritual, emotional, mental process is also being set in place. At this time you receive a spiritual, emotional imprint that your body will use all its life. It only takes twelve days for this imprinting process to be completed, but other systems take longer to reach full development. During this period, you receive a cellular structure that consists of trillions of cells. Each cell has a memory and has its own energy. Cells have a level of light and dark energy. Light chromosomes sometimes link with dark chromosomes. When this takes place, there are weak links that create problems with the development of the body. We want Light cell linkage, and, of course, we pray for that. We want our new babies, our new conceptions, to have total Light linkage. In most cases, unfortunately, we get what is passed on from our progenitors because this was not a consideration to even be prayed for.

"Some gene imprints from the father and mother do not always come together perfectly. There are many defects in combining the genes from two parents. This is not a mistake. It is what we are to deal with in our life time. This is where fracturing conflicts of neuron circuits and alienation in those fractured areas is identified. Problems that are created in structure might be illnesses or vascular irregularity. These can be mental or emotional disorders, disease, or structural problems.

"Some people develop multiple personalities. This can be from abuse that progenitors suffered in their early years. Then they passed forward all the emotion to you in your cells. These are called *Progenitor Cells*. Some of these cells are very powerful! Very early in life, even in the womb, progenitor cells learn ways to re-live their past life experiences and take over portions of the thinking power of the brain and body they have come to. They relive their negative emotions and thoughts vicariously as part of life as if it was now. They act out one or more personalities, which are not found, except by Muscle Testing (MT). I will explain this later.

"The personality disorder in some people is not found and many cells can act out, take over. Sanity is lost to this person without the help of prayer, a good practitioner, and the Integration.

"When identified, the personality progenitor cells will lose their dark, take-over power. They are no longer able to activate in the mind. The cells are asked to be cleansed by the Light of God and neutralized to become inert energy. Thereafter, they will create good energy for the body with no ability to take over the mind, ever again if they do not accept Light energy. ***They must be cut away. The angels will take them as they leave.***

"Also, because of DNA, a person may receive bone structure characteristics from someone in the progenitor line and look just like that person. One may have the same face structure as Aunt Annie or the same type of hair and height as great Uncle Tom.

"Physical characteristics are not the only characteristics contained in DNA. We also receive emotional patterns, mental and spiritual patterns with the capacity to love, receive miracles, abundance, joy, charity, hope, faith, and many, many more characteristics.

"In the genetic makeup, people receive both good and bad characteristics from their parents' genetic lines. For example, if one of your ancestors became a horse thief or a saint then the propensity for you to become a thief or saint is implanted into your personal DNA and subsequently is passed forward in energy to your offspring for untold generations. *Likewise, the way our ancestors lived and even the way **we live our***

lives now *may affect future generations forever in the family line."*

The King went on to explain, "You also influence your genetic inheritance and your cells by how you think and the words you say. You will create positive or negative outcomes in your life and the lives of others by how you treat yourself and your children. How you think and what you say to yourself by *Word or by Word thought* affects the cells in your body. All word thought creates energy, which is stored in the cells and is passed forward in the embryo during the days of creation after conception.

"When you think one negative thought or say one negative word, it resounds into the subconscious at 1,000 repeats per minute. This thought will connect to the other negative cells having the same or similar thoughts. You are then what is called a Negative person. It is much better to connect to the positive word thought cells that are of God's Love and Light. This brings a positive, higher level of thinking. Thus, the scripture in Genesis: 'And the Word became flesh..." (John 1:14).

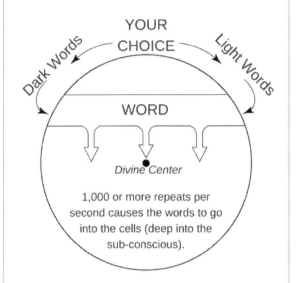

THE HUMAN CELL
YOU BECOME YOUR WORD

YOUR
CHOICE

Dark Words

Light Words

WORD

Divine Center

1,000 or more repeats per
second causes the words to go
into the cells (deep into the
sub-conscious).

Positive words connect us to God the Father of Light. This moves the WORD connection down to the DIVINE CENTER. When functioning in the Divine Center, there is instant spiritual guidance. Everything works in the Light as connections to God.

"Your emotional, mental, physical and spiritual blueprint is being formed in the first two months after conception. These days are called Embryo Days. By the twelfth day, your mind and heart are almost complete. Every part of you is in place, already becoming special, magnificent you.

"***There is no one like you anywhere in the world. You have become your own unique design, selected from hundreds, even thousands of progenitors.***

"All the embryo does from then on is grow, finish the circuitry, and gain weight!

"Your *own Intelligence* has existed forever. It took charge with God's help at the creation of your body. It *injects* itself into the physical creation in embryo on or before the third week of development. The intelligence now has a strong influence as to what you will become. If the entire embryo comes together perfectly, you will have a perfect life, perfect health, and be a perfect child. Unfortunately, that rarely happens.

☙

TWINS

"During conception, twins are conceived more often than not. If early in the pregnancy one of the twins is sloughed off as a clot, dissolved or reabsorbed by the mothers body, the remaining embryo twin develops and is born with others not knowing of the twin. The baby born may have several unsolved problems or experience Phantom Twin programs at some time in their life. This means they are troubled, trying to find answers for duality with self judgment and grief at being alive.

"Whether the same or opposite gender, the surviving twin will have adjustments. This might be the fear of being left alone again by the same or opposite sex. There are emotional disorders of loneliness, rejection, and being the wrong gender. The surviving twin will have to work through these emotional barriers at some time in his or her life. These are some examples of phantom twin programs.

"A *maternal twin* is a monozygotic conception, meaning the release of one egg fertilized by one sperm. This instantly divides making two embryos. This creates identical twins that are a perfect mirror image reproduction of each other. This set of twins shares the same amniotic fluid and sac. They share the same placenta and umbilical cord, as well as the same DNA they received at the time of their great division. The only difference is their spirit. Each spirit has its own individual identity, male or female, patterned as a spirit child of God. Their own individual spirit enters the body sometime before or during the time of birth, giving yet another dimension to the pattern of life. They have the same perfect physical pattern in every way, and yet their own identity.

"Fraternal Twins are produced from two eggs each fertilized by a different sperm.

"This is two or more singular conceptions at one time in the same womb. Although conceived at the same time as the other embryo, it has its own sac, placenta and amniotic fluid with its own umbilical cord. Each twin has a different DNA, chromosome and genetic patterning with each one having its own looks, structure, and coloring. They are completely different from each other.

"If you have been a twin in the womb, the debilitating programs can take place and are planted deep in core energy. This negative programming takes place when one twin does not grow or is lost. There are many problems for the living child to work through and resolve. Most input has to do with self-worth, guilt and being the right one to be alive now. The twin left in the womb often becomes a care taker, trying to claim strength from sadness and loss created by the inability to save the life of their loved one, the unknown twin.

"All of the first programming of 100,000 to 500,000 neurons uploaded daily in the womb are done at the time of loss. Depending on the number of days the twins were together, it can be very traumatic for the one remaining to go on living. This is why it is important to identify this point of creation."

ॐ

PRAYER

"Courtney and Jennifer," said the King, "clear messages *may be sent by clearings in the form of a dedicated prayer. This blessing is carried to the person you love by the Light of God.* The clearing prayer then is received by your loved one.

"If not accepted immediately, it wraps around them in their energy like a shawl. Eventually, as they pass through a growth pattern and accept themselves more completely, this clearing may be accepted by them on some level, at some time. It is there waiting for them and will go in to their core energy at the perfect time.

"However, the Integration prayer must connect to some Light that is already in the person prayed for.

"The spirit of truth may become lost by allowing someone else to decide their choices or if they continually make a choice for darkness.

LAW OF ABUNDANCE -
Change your vibration through prayer

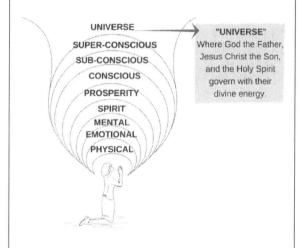

"Ask, and it shall be given you; seek, and ye shall find; knock and it shall be opened unto you..." (Matthew 7:7)

God and the Integration will clear all energy to Worth, Deserve and Receive by your own clearness and connection to God and the Universe through prayer.

"Truth can be lost to the point of no recognition by living lies that they know are lies and by ignoring the truth. It can be lost by not standing up for truth or claiming it in all areas of their life.

"However, there is always repentance and coming to the Lord in prayer with all their hearts.   But they must be able to accept the prayer as from, 'Light to Light.'

"Most souls, even though they appear totally dark, have a shred of light left in them.

"Making choices of darkness and being away from the light for a long time can and does remove sensitivity to recognizing the truth. The Integration, with prayer, will help open them to truth again; and if there is any light left on any level, the work for them can be complete."

The King then let them see in the form of laser-like connections, the loving, earnest prayers being formulated and sent to others. The prayers originated by connecting to God's Love that is the Light, by saying, "Dear God, the Eternal Father." This is the beginning of the connecting prayer to the Light.   This is how to address God. Then say by saying the name of the person for whom the prayer is being created. This is an instant light, laser beam connection!   This Light is brighter, cleaner and clearer than your modern lasers. The laser Light connection from all who are praying together is an instantaneous bond.

"Where several people or an entire congregation are praying for one person, the light from each prayer will merge and blend together, becoming a very powerful, enormous, connected beam. As this powerful Light of God goes to the person being prayed for, that person is filled up, surrounded, bathed, strengthened, repaired, protected, and restored by this Light.

"Some of the beams are larger, stronger and more powerful than others. This has to do with the level of faith, knowledge, and confidence of the person praying. In other words, they know who they are calling upon. Calling upon the Powers of Heaven is done by anyone, as God honors all prayers, however they are said, or by whomever they are said. But an acquired knowledge of faith, prayer and experience from **many** answered prayers creates a strong testimony of God's Love.

"When all the prayers being said for others was made visible, it looked like trillions of light laser beams being connected to one another, creating a web of Light around the world and always bonded to God.

"The thickest beams are from large groups of people who are praying for one person. Then, when millions of people pray for a sick or lost child, the beam is gigantic. God knows the earnest prayers of those who love Him and who love children. He knows those who pray for and care for children, and they will be blessed.

"There was a child with the name 'Smart' that the world prayed for. The beam of Light for her was enormous. It came in from all over the world, and she was found safe!"

The King said, "Prayer and the Integration sent to a person will help that person delete negative programs that have caused them to have problems in their life. This is called a long distance clearing.

"Jennifer, your sister shares the same DNA structure as you. Do this: pray and Integrate. Then ask God to give the work you have done for yourself, to her.

"Deuteronomy 5:9 says, 'the sins of the fathers are visited upon the heads of the children to the third and fourth generation.' Using the Integration, God will cleanse all the sins of the fathers and mothers to the third and fourth generation forward and backward in your genealogy line just because you have made the effort to do this clearing.

"The Integration releases negative energies brought into our bodies. There also is the DNA programming which can be illness, depression or sadness. This can all be released by holding the image of the person, your sister in this case, clearly in your mind, connecting yourself to God, then integrating.

"In other words, Jennifer, say this: 'Heavenly Father, in the name of Jesus Christ, I ask that all the work that has been done to clear my DNA be given to my sister!' Close your eyes and hold the image of your sister clearly in your mind as you integrate for her in the attitude of prayer. Tap with your right hand one tap on the forehead, then one tap on the thymus. Then, put that same hand on your heart. Hold for a second, then do positive affirmations. When this is completed, ask to now be disconnected from her energy. This will allow the prayer to be your functioning program, as well as hers.

☙

MUSCLE TESTING

The King continued, "Muscle testing is used to search the conscious, subconscious and super conscious mind for broken programs, for weaknesses, inability, illness, mental and emotional brokeness. Your body is your computer. It knows all the answers. It is a truth barometer. When the subconscious and the conscious are in harmony with God, the body will give 99% true and correct answers. The other 1% is from the way you ask the question to be tested. When not in harmony with God, the body becomes weak. The strength or weakness can be found by yes and no answers and by testing a set of muscles. This is called *body kinesiology*."

He said, "Let me show you how muscle testing is done. Extend your right arm, Jennifer. Clear your space. Think of being immersed in White Light. Now, say a truth."

Jennifer said, "My name is Jennifer."

"Now, Courtney, try to pull her arm down."

Jennifer's arm stayed strong and in place.

"Truth makes you strong. Now, Jennifer, say a falsehood."

Jennifer said quickly, "My name is Joan."

Courtney tested Jennifer's arm again. Immediately her arm dropped to her side.

The King said, "Our Inner God Self, Inner Spirit, Inner I AM, Inner Energy, or whatever name you choose to call this special part of yourself it connects with the central nervous system and registers in the autonomic response of the muscle system.

"The muscles become strong with truth and weak with falsehood or dishonesty.

"The muscles in your body act according to your subconscious, innermost thoughts. The subconscious also governs autonomic response to all the systems in your physical body. It brings up emotions to be solved, then mentally puts us into chaos if we do not work it out. Through the muscle system the Spirit as the God-connection, can answer what is best and right for us consciously, when our energy is cleared to the Light.

"Kinesiology identifies weaknesses by muscle strength. This kinesiology is called Muscle Testing (MT). When used with the Integration, it lets change happen. After the MT search is done and you find weaknesses, integrate for instant change and increased strength."

He cautioned, "*Always make a statement rather than ask a question.* The subconscious doesn't recognize a statement that begins with a question.

"Stay realistic. Because the future is changeable, it is best to not use this testing to predict or ask questions about the future. It will often be wrong because the future is unpredictable. The future can change and make whatever you are testing obsolete in a very short while.

"Pray and clear your space. Then MT by stating, "I am 100% in the Light of God, now! My body is willing to give 100% true, accurate and correct answers according to the will and love of God?" Then make statements such as: each segment of your developmental stages."

"Make statements such as: 'I am 100% in the Light of God. Now!'

"Not Question: 'Am I in the Light of God 100%?'

"Weaknesses will be determined by MT or using an arm or any of your muscle systems to find *where the problem began*. Ask to go to the *deepest level* of input. Other muscle systems may be used. I will leave this information with you as you continue to study later.

"Go through each phase of development in the following order. Always look for *strength*. If the muscle tests strong, there is no problem. When the muscle tests weak, you have *located a problem*. The brain does a search for a core program in the subconscious, always *going backward* through major periods from *maturity to your first creation*. To make sure you have covered all the stages, use the order of going from the present to the past:

- From age eighteen to five, to one year, if one year breaks with weakness, shift to Months.
- 12 months to birth. At times the shift will be to weeks and days.
- Fetal development back to two months in embryo.
- Conception through twelve days of embryo development
- DNA Mother and DNA Father
- Twelve energy centers, counted as 1, 2, 3, etc. up to 12. This includes 12 levels of energy in each center.
- 12 dimensions, twelve levels in each dimension.

146

- ♦ Spiritual creation
- ♦ Intelligence
- ♦ Worlds
- ♦ Back to your first creation
- ♦ Infinity and Forever."

The King continued to explain, "If any one or all of these areas are weak, integrate and ask God the Eternal Father, in the name of His Son Jesus Christ of Nazareth, to heal the weak areas through the Holy Spirit. The integration works well only with prayer. The integration will erase most undesirable core programs, no matter what, or put anything you choose to have changed into remission and balance.

"I will also leave you a list of processes to work through later to help you search and integrate. I suggest you do no more than three or four every three days. So as not to become overloaded with change and be confused for a while. You may notice differences immediately or it may take a few days or weeks before you notice the transformation. You will become more balanced and calm. This is your responsibility as a child of God to clear your energy of darkness and negative thinking.

This is part of the law of Eternal Progression in which you now live and always have.

The King continued, "Your subconscious is a massive computer. *Only God can clear it. The integration belongs to him.*

"You see, according to the strength of your faith, you will be able to ask God to move mountains. (Luke 17:6.)

"Because of negative words and thoughts, DNA, weak genetics or trauma, many weaknesses can by-pass our strength in faith. Then, we have very little strength left of our faith to move those mountains. The Integration deletes the negatives and releases you to your stronger, fuller faith. This is why God gave the Integration to us. When we use the Integration, we become stronger and fuller in our faith. With layers of blocks and fractures removed from our physical, emotional, mental, and spiritual bodies, we can then have perfect faith.

"**God and all His forces of Light angels will be with you as you learn to Integrate and grow.**

"This earth's aura or atmosphere is the darkest of any of the planets. In this darkness live many dark entities. All these forces of darkness and evil attach to negative thought because it is a form of words.

Negative thought cannot exist in light and can only find a place to belong in dark energy.

* This may come through your television into your home.
* Perhaps your mate or someone you work or live with is a negative person.
* Many dark forces are connected to each and every negative thought or word.

"But when we are in God's Light and truth, dark forces have nowhere to connect because they cannot connect to God's Light." the King said.

"I will leave you now. I have been on an assignment to help you. Your prayers are always heard. **You are now charged with an assignment to get these truths and this information to the people you love. It has the capacity to change the world, one person at a time.**"

Illya, the King's daughter, stepped toward Courtney and Jennifer. She told them this story:

"When I was sixteen, I watched a man die. Humans usually do not have the gift of seeing spirits leave their earth bodies in death, but I did! I made an interesting observation at the time. I saw that the new body was covered with a dark, cotton-like substance which slipped from his body and landed in a circle at his feet until it was almost knee-deep. Then, I could see the beautiful colors of the new body form, which were brighter than those colors on earth. I didn't understand what it meant then, but I do now.

"This body form that I observed is our spirit, which lives inside our body, then leaves our body at death. It gives life and energy and is pure and precious matter. If we were to see our spirit, it would look just like us.

"We contaminate our spirit by what we take into our body by way of food, water, substances, chemicals, thoughts, and the air we breathe. The cotton-like substance that fell from Derth's spirit body represents acid foods and toxic substances that were ingested. Toxins are not part of the spirit world. They remain on earth. Some substances such as tobacco, alcohol, drugs, and chemicals can make our spirit toxic or even cause a spiritual addiction. There are spirits who do not go to the Light because they want more of what they are addicted to. So they stay on the earth trying to get their addiction satisfied in any way. They do not know that God can and does heal addictions.

"How you care for your body and what you eat is very important. Your energy level will fluctuate from having lots of energy to extreme tiredness, depending on the food and water you consume. For high energy, it is best to keep your body in an alkaline state with your stomach and intestines being acid. It is important to eat foods that make your body become alkaline but not too alkaline, 8.2 pH is good.

A microscope was designed to magnify up to one hundred times greater than the object being viewed. It was used in a class of twenty five to show the content of a blood cell.

During a break, the hematologist said, "This is not part of the class, but I want to show what I have been experimenting on. It has to do with prayer and the Light."

He adjusted his microscope that a normal size apple would fit under the lens. Immediately an enormous apple was on the screen in front of us. It was a red apple, nothing different or strange about it other than it filled the screen.

The class was told to pray for the apple like a blessing on the food. "Thank God for this apple, please bless it with Light, health and strength." Immediately the apple began to glow with energy like a light bulb had been turned on inside of it. The Light expanded from inside the apple to the outer most regions of the screen

Being amazed at the example of prayer and the power of prayer on food, do you bless your food? How about your life? A visual example is worth a thousand words. I now know what happens when a blessing is said on the food. It literally changes the molecules to Light.

"Always pray and give thanks for your food. Ask that your food be blessed and magnified with Light energy to bring forth more light that will satisfy the needs of the body. This changes the food by giving it increased pH-balanced power.

"It is important to drink water which has been filtered, alkalized, ionized and is no less than 7.2 pH balanced. One may also bless the water you drink. I will give you some guidelines to help you keep your body full of energy and in a pH-balanced state."

The light in the room faded. Courtney and Jennifer looked at one another and realized the magnitude of what they had been given. Lying beside them on the table was a stack of papers. As they examined the papers, they found information for healing every type of illness and emotional problem and how to integrate each one. This list had been formulated by the King and Illya and had been left to assist Courtney and Jennifer in their assignment.

The King left enough information to help these women understand more fully how to find, process, and enrich their lives. Here is that information. It will help everyone learn how to live life in tune with God, bringing to them success, happiness, health and profound Light.

☙

The Be Light and Shine
Clear-ology
processes are brought to you through
Janet Taylor

༁

LEFT BRAIN-RIGHT BRAIN BALANCE

The brain is all powerful. There are many parts of the brain, but two parts are what we work with the most: the sub-conscious and the conscious. They are the link to the Left and Right sides. The sub-conscious stores feelings, pictures, images, and past and present thoughts. It also stores negative memories such as pornography and other unrighteous thoughts. These will come up into the conscious mind repeatedly. This does influence present time events. All of this information is stored in the sub-conscious. When something happens in the present time that stimulates an old emotion, thought, or memory, it will come out of storage and influence a reaction to the event as though it is in the present. In this way it takes charge of the body's actions and emotions. These mental images are the, drivers that make the mind and body act out. At times it can be unpleasant.

Think of the sub-conscious as a memory storage bin for 90% of all that has ever happened to you. In fact, when you talk, the cells in your body act out what you are saying. When you think visualized thoughts, you are really talking to your own sub-conscious. Whatever you say out loud or to yourself will happen! The sub-conscious will see that you get gifted in the present what you say or think. Consciously, you won't know this is happening. This is a silent thought process that is always acted out in the conscious and played in present time. In other words, when you talk, the cells of your body listen to what you are saying. Then the brain is the computer that puts it all into action.

The sub-conscious holds the memory of not only every positive experience but also all the negative ones. Over time, these have created who you are. Because of all your characteristics, weaknesses, and beliefs about yourself, there may come a time in your life when you want to change negative habits and get rid of old beliefs because they don't serve you anymore and cause problems instead.

To be able to change this massive computer is an enormous concept. It can only be changed through the Light and the power of God. This is done through prayer, Light, meditation, holding your left hand over the top of your brain and Integrate. After the Integration has helped rid you of negative emotions and thoughts, always say positive affirmations to fill the empty space with Love and Light. Do this daily or the negative will slowly creep back and fill the space again, leaving you then back where you started.

Not only does the brain have a conscious and a sub-conscious, it also has a right and left side, divided right down the middle. Your body wants these two hemispheres to have balanced energy. When the brain is balanced, you will be energized.

When you have a foggy mind, can't think straight, fall asleep when you need to be awake and alert or are absent minded, your brain is out of balance. When energy is low or absent on one side of the brain, the brain is in lockdown. (People who are bipolar, lethargic, or manic will appreciate this process of helping the brain to balance.)

This process takes the good, sweet, patient, loving, kind self (the true you) into both sides of the brain. All the negative aspects of yourself will be erased. Through prayer and *Integration*, balance is restored and magnified The light and balance you feel is love. When you are Love, you are whole.

❧

LIGHT IS LOVE, THE ENERGY OF GOD

Our energy is much like an onion. There are layers and layers of pictures, emotions, and feelings stored in our subconscious. It is released by recognition, then healed with prayer and the Integration.

You may clear the same experience or similar ones several times, only in a different way. When clearing and integrating, the releases will continue to formulate over time. When all that needs to heal surfaces, wholeness and love will become what you are. For some it is immediate. For others it takes longer...perhaps one week to even a year. Your thinking processes will become clear with peace and joy. This will be the result of your efforts.

A professor who taught anatomy at a noted university said, "Mankind has tried to build computers to copy the human mind. There are computers now that will do almost anything. Yet mankind is light years away from understanding the many complex areas of the brain".

Remember, the sub-conscious part of the brain holds as much information as a 10-story building, filling a large city block. The conscious mind is just a little box on top. Quite a difference! No wonder our balance gets out of kilter.

When we understand how immense and ancient we are, how gigantic is the challenge of the Be Light work. We claim the need to become balanced and stay balanced. As we apply the principles of the Integration, we get to clear our personal computers of negative programs. Then, our positive programs become our strongest energy. Balance is personal power. This power stays with us through daily work, applying knowledge, and using the spirit of God.

This power is registered in our aura energy in colors. When our body has balanced energy centers, it gives strong and clear colors. When confused and disturbed, the colors, will be pastel. There may be brown, black or both in the energy field. Being positive and staying in tune with God gives us strong, balanced color. This balanced color may extend outward for hundreds of thousands of miles around us. The stronger the balance, the stronger the power of color.

ॐ

An Example of the Sub-Conscious

It was observed in the Islands, that when one monkey washed its banana, soon all the monkeys were doing the same thing, not only on one island, but also on all of the islands. How did that happen?

Another example, in a large field there were thousands of sheep. Every one of them had its head to the north and its tail to the south. How did each of them know to stand in the same direction?

Animals live in the sub-conscious. They know our thought-energies without us having to say a word. Most animals feel energy of intent and communicate in their own way. Therefore, they seem to be energetically balanced so their intent radiates outward to others on the same level. In a flash, all energy will know the intent.

When we have enough positive energy and Light existing on this earth, it will change to match paradise and be peacefully the same. Just as the monkeys knew to wash their banana and the sheep stood all the same direction, this Light energy will usher in the millennium where we will know perfect peace for a thousand years. We will all be turned to face God, much like the sheep in the field. His Light will be everything as every knee will bow and every tongue confess that Jesus is the Christ, the Light of the world, the Son of God. (Philippians 2:10-11, John 8:12).

Our pure, beautiful spirit, blended with our purified body and the spirit of Christ, will bring us to our wholeness, our balance. We open that door to our wholeness by being *honest*. Our Word has to be as our God! *Without Truth, the physical body is always out of balance.* We, at one time in our creation, agreed that we would find this critical balance of honesty and faith, in order to know and become as our God. In this way we will find our way back to Him while upon this earth. When we fuse our spirit body and our mortal body with truth, prayer and the Integration, we will have strongly balanced energy.

With this balanced energy, the right and left hemispheres of the brain will stop separating. New cross-brain patterns will form. We will know how God thinks and begin to understand what wholeness means for us. When we find the wholeness of God and really know that we are a God in embryo, then we will know Light and Love as the true nature of God.

The right and left parts of the brain have different functions. At our conception we received all our father's progenitor cellular energy in our left brain DNA.

We are given our mother's progenitor cellular energy in our right brain DNA. At times it is mixed but will clear when worked with and integrated.

A cross-brain pattern is established sometime in embryo during the basic setup of genetics. It is behind the nasal area and is called a cross brain patterning. This means the left brain, usually located on the left side of the head takes care of the right side of the body. The right brain takes care of the left side of the body. Usually, this is how our brain patterns are established. This creates balance for the body. A vertical set-up is clumsy with discordant actions.

If functioning correctly, the right brain energy is loving, gentle, creative, emotional feeling, and sees in color. The right brain is creative and referred to as feminine.

If functioning correctly, the left brain is analytical, structured, sees in black and white, works with numbers, is geometric, organized and considered masculine. Thus, we have both female and male attributes within us. To be equally balanced in these attributes is the key to wholeness.

A client named Harry was conceived with his brain registering backwards. The energy of his right and left brain were on opposite sides. His soft gentle side was in the left brain, and the energy of the right brain was structured, rigid and acted out as testy, picky, and unfaithful.

He was bi-polar. Those with him always wondered which side he was going to revolve to in the present. When Harry was acting out his bipolar energy in his right brain, he had the energy of his father who was a very kind, balanced, loving, forgiving, always fair, and devoted man. However, he could switch in a matter of minutes from one side of the brain to the other. This is called bi-polar or manic mood swings. In seconds, he would become a fighting person with no trust, becoming mean, critical and judgmental.

If you are reading this and have this changing energy, this process is important and will help you.

C3

CLEAR-OLOGY PROCESS

Clear-ology means being *one with God*. You must feel the truth of the *Light* or know that the *Light* coming to you is from *God, the Eternal Father.* *God* must be the connection, your Highest Power. This is called, Hooking Up, *clearing yourself* or your space, and anyone you are actively involved with or are working on.

Pray and visualize the *Light* coming to you. Think of it coming to the top of your head as a shaft, beam, or column of light. Visualize its size. Make it large because you want it to stream down through your body to below your feet, filling you and your space.

Then, as you visualize the Light in you, through you, and around you, ask for *balance* to be in your body, mind, and spirit. Balance means alignment or becoming one with God's energy.

We need not fear any other energy because God's energy is everything...a tremendous, powerful peace.

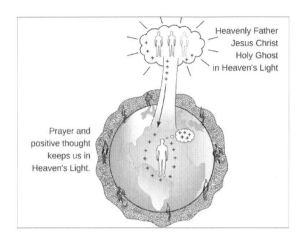

When you image *God* as a Supreme and *Perfect Father*, He will automatically give you His beautiful Light energy. He is perfect. He will never change or die. He was, is, and always will be the supreme, powerful, perfect, unchanging, understanding God...our Eternal Father in Heaven. This is: **White Light, or the Energy of Pure Love.**

His energy fills the universe; and White Light from His energy will come to our aid when we ask, image, or think it to come to us. According to your faith, you can have all you want. This is hooking up!

We all want to function productively every day; but we are susceptible to, and influenced by, unseen negative energies that most people never imagine, see, or even acknowledge.

The veil between the unseen and seen is very thin. Our thoughts draw to us, yes, even pull through the veil to us, what we are thinking.

An attack by dark energy includes disorientated thought, non-productive functioning, depression, dark thinking, and hopelessness. When we think negative thoughts about ourself or someone else, we open ourself up to these negative energies. We must be careful what we think or say to ourself. There may be a whole group of dark energies that accompany you because of negative thoughts.

Also, when we keep company with people who are darkened souls, we take on their negative energy. When we are strong in our clearings, we can clear the darkness from them and us by prayer and visualizing the Light. Teach others to do the same.

We simply need to know that to do this energy work, we must pray for His Light to connect to us. It is essential to know that God the Eternal Father, Jesus Christ and the Holy Spirit are the only authorities here on earth.

There is no other energy that has the power to subdue all other energies other than Jesus Christ. He, alone, is the protection from all unseen entities and dark forces.

After the prayer for clearing and hooking up, make a statement such as: "My flesh is now willing to give 100% true and correct answers according to my spirit and to God's will." Then muscle test.

In this way, the energy influencing the responses from muscle testing, thoughts, feelings, and spiritual input are from God. Our own energy must be clear enough to blend as closely as possible with the energy of our Savior's Light. This procedure is easy to learn and must be done repeatedly.

We are imperfect people. We live on this earth where we are continually buffeted by right and wrong choices and influenced by dark energy. We do not always make the right choices. In order to have the spirit of God reside with us, *repentance* has to be a continual process. Recognizing what we have done wrong and making amends for it must be sincere. It is essential to ask daily for a connection to truth and light. It will be a blessing in your life and in the lives of others. Angels will attend you, and you will experience changes and growth that will surprise and delight you. **This is Clear-ology!**

℘

THE STEPS

Touch the left side of your head with your left hand. MT by using the method you like best and count from 1-10. (1-10 means 10% up to 100% of clear energy. It is easier to count from 1-10 instead of 10-20-30 to 100%.) Pray and ask for clear energy. As you count from one to ten, the muscles will go weak when you have found the current % of energy. Low means under the count of 8 (80%); and if it is low, it is locked on one side of the brain. Integrate!

Touch the right side of your head with your left hand. Muscle test on a scale of 1-10.. As you count from 1-10, again the muscles will go weak when you have found the low energy. If it is under 8; Integrate! This will bring the energy up to a 10.

Place your left hand across the top of your head and MT for neuron exchange. This is the ability to feel (right brain) and analyze (left brain) at the same time. MT from 1-10. As you count from 1 to 10, the muscles will go weak when you have found the low energy under 8. Integrate! This will bring the energy up to a 10 or 100 %.

Say positive affirmations such as, "I am connected to God's energy." "I am balanced." "I am whole." "I am energized." "My body and mind are willing to give 100% true and correct answers according to the will of God." Keep integrating until you have a strong muscle test.

⚘

LOST SOUL HEALING

The energy that surrounds the earth is a dark veil. We don't realize it is there except for how we feel when that darkness is near. Those who are gifted to see energy, actually do see the darkness of this space. This "veil" of darkness exists between the physical world and the spiritual. It surrounds the earth. This dark energy belongs to Lucifer and his host of souls who were cast out of Father's Kingdom, or Heaven, during the war in Heaven. They are referred to as demons, entities or dark souls (*Revelations, 13*).

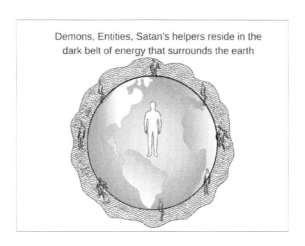

Demons, Entities, Satan's helpers reside in the dark belt of energy that surrounds the earth

On the edge of the veil are tunnels of Light that go from the earth, through the darkest area, to the space where God and angels reside. These tunnels of Light belong to Heavenly Father. So, when spirits come to the earth either as angels or to be born, they can pass through the tunnel of Light and not be confounded by the darkness.

Also, when people leave this life, they are to go to the tunnel of Light to enter Paradise and live in peace, having made a choice of Light and Christ.

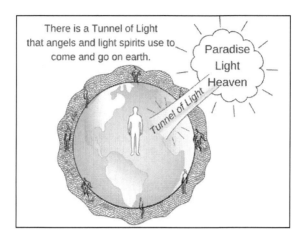

There is a Tunnel of Light that angels and light spirits use to come and go on earth.

Paradise
Light
Heaven

Tunnel of Light

There are souls that don't choose, for some reason, to go to the Tunnel of Light. They either did not know it was there or they chose to stay on the earth in this lowest physical energy because of addiction, another person, or some other reason. Thus, they are named Lost Souls. They aren't especially dark, but they haven't chosen Light. They only know that they are afraid of the demons, entities, and monsters that attack them in that darkness. They know that White Light is better, so they attach to anyone who has a greater Light than the darkness.

When you begin to think thoughts that are not your own, feel weighed down like there is pressure around you and on you that you can't explain, one or more of these lost souls is probably trying to attach to you and borrow your Light energy. You can clear yourself of them. This will help them be released to the Light. The earthbound lost souls need to know there is something else for them to do than be in the earth's physical energy.

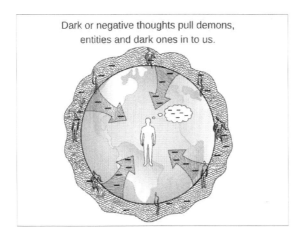

Dark or negative thoughts pull demons, entities and dark ones in to us.

First, teach them about Jesus and the plan of salvation.

Second, teach them about Paradise. Talk mind to mind with them. Tell them that they missed their directions. They do not have to be here. Even Jesus went to Paradise. Paradise is like a big University where you go to be with those who are just like you.

There you also are presented a plan to help you continue your spiritual growth.

Third, ask Father to bring the window of Light over to where you are. The window will immediately appear. Have them look upward and find the opening to this window. This window is called the Tunnel of Light. This is the opening that will take them to a place of refuge and peace. It will take them through the dark energy that surrounds the earth. The tunnel is safe and the dark entities cannot go in there. Jesus Christ himself is the keeper of the opening. He will greet them as they come through the tunnel. They may also find loved ones who have gone before them. Often relatives will be at the window to greet the lost soul and go through the tunnel with them.

Usually, they leave and go through the tunnel. If they do not, it's because they are frightened or they don't understand something about the process. This is when you will reassure them that it is safe to go into the window, then the tunnel. They will have a happy reunion with Jesus and loved ones.

When the earthbound Lost Souls are taught about the window of Light and about Jesus and the Plan of Salvation, there may be many others who are listening to what is taught. These are also lost souls. There may be hundreds that want to go to the Light, but haven't. (The reasons vary considerably.) The window will stay open until all the earthbound souls in the area are in Paradise. They may usher through for days or even weeks. When all are safely through to the other side, the window will close.

A gentleman in his fifties who lived alone expressed the feeling that he had a ghost in his house. He said when he went to bed at night there was a presence on the other side of the bed. He knew someone was there but didn't recognize who it was. He thought maybe it was his dead wife.

When accessed, it was a large, overweight woman with frizzy, red hair. She was saying, "Get out of here! This is my space and you cannot have it! I like it here and it belongs to me!"

When she realized that she was seen and heard, a conversation ensued.

She had attached to this good gentleman at a dance for older people. She liked his Light, went home with him and took up residence with him. As she talked, it was learned that she had died quickly in the 1800's. She had been wandering the earth since then, using other people for her Light source.

When asked if she had a place where she could go and have all the Light she wanted to make her feel good continually, would she go there? She said yes!

The Tunnel of Light was explained and she was told to look up and find it. She automatically started moving toward it as she liked the beautiful Light. As she went through the opening, she turned and waved good bye.

To release Lost Souls to the Light, they need to know that there is something else for them to do other than be on earth. Earth is a scary place when not in the Light. Dark demons and entities try to get these souls to join the dark army. Many do! Others like Light too much to go further into the darkness. They become afraid and attach to anyone who has more Light than they do.

Katrina's mother was oriental. She did not know, understand, nor had ever been taught the purpose of life and how it must blend with Jesus Christ. Katrina took care of her in the last weeks before she died of cancer. Katrina was helped through her personal grief of the loss of her mother by *Clear-ology*.

Three days after the funeral Katrina was found sobbing in her office. She said she could hear her mother sobbing and screaming with fear but could not find her. She did not know where her mother was. Three days she had not slept because her mother was so upset.

From the experience in this book, I knew I have a gift to see and talk to those on the other side of the veil. All I needed to do at this point is ask my Father in Heaven, "Please, allow me see!" This took place immediately!

I saw her mother with both arms wrapped around Katrina's neck screaming in her ear. I said to her by telepathy, "I see you, I hear you! What are you afraid of?"

After she settled from the shock of my connection to her, that I saw her, she began to tell her tale. She wanted to be in the Light, but everywhere she went was Dark. Pointing her right arm and finger outside of the room, she said, "They want to take me with them!"

I looked out of the room and saw very gross, dark ugly creatures along the edge of the room. "They scare me," she said, "and I don't want them to take me!"

I asked her if she knew Jesus Christ. She said, "No."

I began to explain about Paradise and Jesus Christ, how and why, he came to this world. I explained that Paradise is like a big university where you learn and grow in understanding and the "Light of Jesus" is ever present. I told her of the Tunnel of Light that is filled with the Holy Spirit. I explained that this tunnel of Light was waiting for her to choose Jesus and go to Paradise by entering it. Also how Angels come to earth and go back to enter the presence of Jesus Christ through this tunnel. I explained how she was now spirit and had the right to choose the Light and go through the tunnel; and every living soul, now dead but spirit, can choose the Light and do this.   All they have to do is look up and find the opening and choose to go in. It looks like a window of Light.

She chose to go to the Light, and immediately she began to leave this earth. She was half way to the window of Light where loved ones and relatives were waiting for her when she stopped and started to come back. I asked her why she had stopped. She didn't want to leave Katrina.

Just then I heard Katrina say, "Don't stop! Go Mother, Go!"

She then turned back around, continued into the Tunnel and was quickly wrapped up in the arms of loving relatives.

Realizing that Katrina had witnessed everything that happened, I asked who the people waiting were. She said her grandmother and an aunt were there and some relatives that were killed in the bombing of Hiroshima. Katrina and I both wept for her Mother to be safe with Jesus and in the Light.

David

D avid woke up early. He had been in jail three days and this morning was better than the first two. He had finally slept for a few hours. For three days he had thought each day would never end. He had been twisted and wracked with a gnawing need for drugs. The pain was so deep that sleep would not come.

Withdrawal left his physical body ravaged, trembling, and weak. His need had been totally out of control. Today, he was doing better. His body was beginning to heal.

"Three days of no drugs," David thought. "My body is realizing it can get by without using."

At times, he almost felt normal. He could even sleep a little. Dare he hope that he could be free of addiction and back to being himself? He was not sure he even knew the person he had been the last six months. What was it that made him try the white powder? He knew he was chancing addiction. That was him, a dare devil who would try anything once. Only this time what he tried got him hooked immediately and he needed more and more. Then he got into big trouble trying to support the addiction. Shame and guilt washed over him. He knew his mother was coming to see him in jail. Even though she had been in a car wreck, guilt washed over him again. Did he upset her so badly that indirectly he had caused the accident?

David had been buying and selling drugs to have money for his own addiction. He had been breaking the law. The more he did, the less he cared. Now that he was getting back to the real him, he knew he was very guilty. He wanted to go straight with no lying this time!

He loved his mother; she was an angel in his life. His father was a good man and an excellent person. They had been good examples to him all his life.

"Why do I always make bad choices?" He asked himself. "Even when I have not wanted to do these horrible things, why have I done them anyway? Oh, Mother and Father, I'm so sorry to cause all this pain and bring shame to myself and to you!"

David pulled his knees up to his chest and sobbed great, shaking sobs from deep within his gut. His tears ran like rivers down his face. As the sobs and tears continued, they brought a clear, vivid realization, like a video to his mind. showing him all that he had done to hurt himself, his family, God, and mankind. Words began to spill from his mouth.

God, are you there?

Do you hear, do you care?

When I cry out in the night

Will you come to ease my fright?

At times you seem so near, then

I'm free from worries, fear.

But now, I'm all alone

I call but no one's home.

But could it be just me?!

Too blind, too proud to see!?

The help you always send

Kind words, or the touch of a friend.

Oh help me Lord to be

More open, aware of thee!

For only through help from

Above, may I find an Inner Love.

(Written 4/26/88 in jail.
Used by permission of the author.)

He then fell from his cot to his knees. "Please, God.   Please, my Savior.   Please, forgive me and help me!"

Instantly!   Immense Light filled the room. He felt strong, gentle arms around him. They were arms that penetrated a depth of love he had never felt before. This unconditional Love filled his whole being. It penetrated through him and surrounded him and everything in the room with Light. A piercing   wave   of   instant   forgiveness cleansed his heart, and he felt loved and cherished just the way he was.

This love conveyed to him all his worth as though he had never done anything wrong. He felt very special, cared for, and strong in that moment.

When he turned to see whose wondrous arms were holding him and loving him, he looked into the eyes of the Savior, who said, **"Go, and sin no more."**

The words pierced David's soul. Then the Savior was gone. He came quickly, and He left quickly. But not without sealing into David's soul a desire stronger than ever to be clean.

David wanted to go with Him because he felt empty without His presence. But he also felt healed. Feeling a very deep sense of gratitude, he realized he no longer felt the need for an earthly stimulant. He wanted to keep the love he now felt. He knew that Jesus had instantly replaced his weaknesses with His powerful love. He also knew he would never use drugs again because of this "mind altering" experience he had just which made him a stronger, faith-filled David.

The passage of time meant nothing to him. As he knelt and re-played the experience over and over in his mind, the rattling sound of keys in the lock of his cell door brought him back to the present. The door opened, and someone said, "David, you're free to go home. Your father is waiting for you."

Again, gratitude flooded over him as he rose to leave the cell. He went down the hall where his dad was waiting with open arms.

David walked right into those most welcome arms. They both wept. For the first time in his life, David understood the love his father felt for him. It experienced so much like the love he had just felt from the Savior.

"I'm making some changes in my life, Dad. You'll see. Dad, did you know that Jesus visits people in jail; and that He loves these people as much as anyone else in the world?"

The Next Week

Courtney was on her way home from shopping when she felt an urge to stop and pay Jennifer a visit. As she pulled her car up to the curb, she noticed a tanned, tall man, probably about her age, mowing the lawn. His t-shirt was tucked into his right back Levi pocket of his pants, it swayed back and forth like a horse's tail hanging out the back of a horse trailer and blown by the wind. She noticed his trim waist and how strong and well-proportioned he was.

Courtney chuckled. "Who is this handsome fellow?" She stared through the car window. "What a build! I wonder how I could meet him. He must be working for Jennifer and Robert."

David felt someone looking at him. He turned to see where that strong energy was coming from.

"Oh, no," thought Courtney as she ducked her head. "I wonder if he saw me staring at him."

☙

David was impressed with the red Nissan parked by the curb. It was shiny and glistened like a mirror. "Whoever owns that car has taken good care of it," David thought. He kept looking to see who was in the car. The car door opened, and a beautiful young woman got out. "Hmm, nice," he thought. "Is she my age?" He noticed her slender, yet well-formed shape, long brown hair and dark eyes. He thought she was the most beautiful woman he had ever seen.

David's knees went weak as her brown eyes connected with his blue ones. He turned the lawnmower off; and with one swift movement, reached for his tee shirt, quickly pulling it over his head. Then he just stood there frozen, tongue-tied, and feeling awkward. In one quick moment, he evaluated his looks. "Am I dirty? Is my hair messed up? Ugh! My hat's on backwards!" He quickly turned it, thinking he had it straight; but it was sideways with the bill over his ear. He could not take his eyes off her!

Courtney smiled and thought, "I wonder if he knows his hat is sideways, and his tee shirt is on backwards, the tags are sticking up under his chin. *Heh, heh."* she chuckled.

With a sunny, quizzical smile, she broke the silence between them, while never taking her eyes from his. "Hi. My name is Courtney."

"You sure do... take good....care of your... car," stammered David.

"Yes," she said. "It's a new car, and I like my car to shine. I work at keeping it clean. I had another red car that I called my Pet. I purchased it about the time the movie Aladdin came out. There was a Red Carpet in the movie and my friends teased me about my Red Car-pet carrying us and flying around...thus, the name, Car-Pet. However, I was in a car wreck and the insurance policy made it possible to replace that car with this one. I like this car, but I really, really loved my first car. It's a good feeling to have a car clear of debt, and I'm trying to think of a good name for it."

"Oh, by the way, my name is David. I have been mowing the lawn for my parents." He extended his hand. "I'll help you think of a name for your car. That will be fun."

As Courtney extended her hand to his, she thought, "This handsome guy is David? He doesn't look like he is in trouble. Is this the same David Jennifer told me about?" Her thoughts tumbled over one another. This David could be the man of her dreams—tall, blue eyed, short blonde hair, now curling around his cap from perspiration, framing his strong, angular face. But most importantly, he looked sweet, clean, normal and wholesome. She noted no tattoos or earrings, and thought, "I wonder if he tells the truth and keeps his word." As her small hand went into his large warm hand, she felt a sense of belonging. Courtney wanted to keep her hand in his. "What is this?" she thought. "I really like him, but I don't really know him."

David liked the warmth of this young woman named Courtney. In fact, he loved her name. He liked her teeth, her lips, her warm smile, and her expressive brown eyes. She was the right size, just past his shoulder. "Probably around 5ft. 6 inches and a nice build, not too heavy, not too light," he thought. Just then, she started to take her hand away. He held on to it a little longer, and with a small tug, tightened his hand a little. He really did not want to let it go.

It seemed their eyes were looking into one another's souls. Courtney thought, "Where is the druggie? I see no sign of him. What happened to change him? He isn't anything like I expected. I like him! I feel I could like him a whole lot more!"

☙

Jennifer noticed that the lawn mower had stopped. Curious, she stepped to the window. She pushed the curtain aside and peered out through the glass.

There was David and Courtney with right hands clasped, looking deeply into one another's eyes, smiling and talking. Jennifer's breath caught, viewing the synergistic energy that radiated from the couple on the lawn. A question automatically formed in her mind, *"Will Courtney one day be my daughter-in-law?"*

"The Gift is from God. Use it with Prayer and the Angels will attend you."

King Enoch

AUTHORS COMMENTS
AND
PERSONAL STORY

Author's Comments

This story is based on real-life experiences. The Integration is real, it has been tried and tested. When implemented with an open heart and mind to the Light and Love of God, it works. It brings tremendous positive change to each individual who uses it.

I now ask you to take charge of your life in every aspect, using the Integration to clear physical, mental, emotional, and spiritual dissention.

Take charge of the leaps of growth that you will find herein.

"Know that actions and consequences are linked together."

Recognize your part in life—how you may have allowed your subconscious memories to program darkness, causing failure.

Take charge of clearing negative programs from your life and physical surroundings.

Complete unfinished projects of unresolved or uncompleted parts of your past.

Resolve to go forth nobly, majestically, and in a manner befitting a Son or Daughter of God honoring "King, God and Prophet Enoch and his Light Angel workers." For that is exactly who you are.

- Choose to overcome the worldly.
- Choose to be whole, complete, and as perfect as possible.
- Choose life!
- Choose to free yourself of substances and people that interfere with your wholeness.

The greatest discovery of any generation is that human beings can alter their lives by altering the attitudes of their mind!
– Albert Einstein

Once you are free of the negative memories and programs of the past, you will be filled with strength. You will look forward to life filled with hope and joy in the present as well as in the future.

Taking charge with this method of release, you will enrich and transform your life.

For the first time, you will find opportunities come to you begging to be lived.

Embrace life entirely----acknowledging the Savior always! And with joy, accept, share and live fully, "The Heavenly Gift."

Author's Personal Story

Early one morning, in Idaho the sun was shining and it was a beautiful day. I was going to a farm twenty miles away to measure the home for carpet and drapes.

I drove almost through the town and was at the edge, when a car pulled out in front of me. I assessed that the driver was not doing well or something was very wrong with him.

As I approached the dam that was used as a bridge, the road curved in a U shape to go over the Snake River. From there, the highway went into a large five mile curve and then straightened out to continue toward the next town.

The driver in front of me kept driving erratically and kept going over the center line. I was fearful he would drive off the road so I laid on my horn trying to get him to wake up and not lose control. But back and forth over the middle line he went anything I did, did not change his behavior. After the long curve the road straightened out and I felt relieved and hoped he could drive better on a road that did not curve.

I panicked as I noticed a large two trailer, white potato truck coming toward us. The driver in front of me went over the line just as the truck began to pass him. His car hit the double wheels on the side of the truck.

It all happened so fast! The car was smashed and tossed like a tattered rag into the ditch on the right side of the road.

The truck couldn't stop as his brakes had been mangled. I jumped from my car and ran to the poor man who was hurt, possibly dying. I have told you the rest of the story. The difference this time in telling you; is that it was a car! The truck driver had a radio to contact the Highway Patrol. It was the Patrol officer who laid his hand on my shoulder, not my father. The left side of the car was torn off with the driver's body hanging from the now removed door opening. The seat belt was the old style; it held him in the car, fastened only on the hips, across his lap. This was where I saw his spirit leave his the body. It happened just the way I described it!

When he comprehended what had happened, instead of falling into a tree, he leaned on and fell backward into the trunk of his car, frantically he pulled himself out. When I returned to the town to write of the crash at the police station, he sat beside me! I was aware all of this and it happened exactly the way I wrote it in the story. No one else was involved. No one else saw this, only me!

My brain went into a frenzy! I can always focus and work, busy is good, so I went ahead and measured carpets and drapes. When finished, I drove the twenty miles home with my brain saying all the way," We did not see that"! I told no one until, I felt crazy! I finally talked to the head of my church. He told me to tell no one! As people would all think something was wrong with me, and think it strange. I carefully did as he said.

Three days later Dennis (by then I knew his name) came to me in spirit and asked me to contact his wife and tell her that he was okay. I did not do that! I saw the officer who handled the case at the grocery store a few days later. He confirmed that I should not tell Dennis's wife anything! She was pregnant with their third baby and was close to having a nervous breakdown. I was weak in my growth then. I let others do my thinking. Now, I don't!

Mrs. Dennis Lefever, I saw your husband die and he is in a wonderful place. He is safe and well. I guess you can say I wrote this book for you.

I wanted to say to the whole world," I am sorry I was so weak in my ability to make decisions. Now with my growth intact, you would have been the only thing that mattered. I hope your children and you have found peace. I pray your world has righted itself and you have been able to move on with your life and be happy. His first and only thoughts were, of you!

~Janet Taylor

RESOURCES

Muscle Testing (Kinesiology) for Information

☙

K inesiology was developed in the 1960's by George Goodhart. This is a study of anatomy and body mechanics in relationship to human behavior. Knowledge of the human mind and body has been developed at quantum leaps since 1960.

Care needs to be given not to use muscle testing beyond its use of internal search for self-knowledge and information on personal past tapes and programs.

The muscle group of an arm or leg or hand is used by pushing gently down while the person resists the push. If the muscle becomes weak or "mushy", then the response is a "no" or "false". If the muscle is "strong", then the response is a "yes" or "true". Muscle testing can be done using different muscle systems of the body. The ones that are most often used are noted with the instructions.

The body's energy systems love truth, and they respond to truth by showing strength. When we live by truth, all of our muscle systems are strong. When we act out or believe a lie, we lose our strength.

Using this method, we are able to muscle test for information

Our Inner God Self, Inner Spirit, Inner I AM, Subconscious Inner Energy, or Spirit or whatever name you choose for this special part of yourself connects with the central nervous system, registering in the autonomic response of the muscle system and all other energy. The muscles become strong with truth and weak with untruth.

The muscles in your body act according to your subconscious innermost thoughts. The subconscious, also governs autonomic response to all the systems in your physical body. It brings up emotion to be solved and mentally throws us into chaos if we do not work with it. Through the muscle system, the Spirit, being the God connection, can answer what is best and right for us consciously when our body is cleared to the Light of God.

Kinesiology identifies weaknesses by muscle strength. This kinesiology is called Muscle Testing. If used with the Integration, it will let change happen. With the MT, a search is done to find weaknesses which can be integrated with instant change and strength returning to the body.

Always make a Statement rather than ask a Question. *The subconscious doesn't recognize a statement beginning with a question. A statement would be begin with, "This is...".*

Pray and clear your space to the Light and truth of God the Eternal Father.

MT by stating, "I am 100% in the Light of God, now!" You then make statements about each segment of your development periods. Weaknesses will be determined by MT, using an arm or any of your muscle systems to find where the problem began. Other muscle systems may be used.

In more technical language, our Inner God self, Inner spirit, Inner I am, or Subconscious Inner energy knows all truth. Our Inner energy connects with the central nervous system that registers in the muscles being tested. When a "no" or "false" truth comes from our inner energy, a subsequent weakening in our overall energy will not support the strength necessary to resist the pressure on the muscle group. When a "yes" or "true" truth comes from within, our muscles receive plenty of energy to resist the push.

> **Because the future is changeable, it is best to never MT to predict or ask questions about the future. It will more often than not end up being wrong. The unpredictable nature of the future can make whatever you are testing obsolete in a short while.**

Muscle testing is used to search the conscious and subconscious mind for broken programs, weaknesses, illness, mental and emotional problems. Your body is your computer. It knows all the answers. It is a truth barometer. When the subconscious and the conscious are in harmony with God, the body will give 99% true and correct answers. The other 1% is the way you ask the question to be tested. When not in harmony with God, the body becomes weak. The strength or weakness is found by yes and no answers by testing one set of muscles. This is called Body Kinesiology.

Statements of truth are always best. Clearing your space before starting is a good assurance of truth. Ask, "I am 100% in truth according to the will of God the Eternal Father."

☙

MUSCLE TEST (MT) PROCEDURE

1. Extend arm. Gently push downward on the Deltoid muscle.
    *   A strong resistance is positive or "yes." A weak or mushy resistance is negative or "no."
2. Tests:
    *   State a truth. MT and check for positive response.
    *   Next, state a falsehood. MT and check for a negative response.
    *   Try several times with different statements. Develop a "feel" for the person's energy.
3. In asking, always make positive statements.
    *   A person may be energized and give all "yes" answers, or experience an energy loss and give all "no" answers. Integrate! Place the right hand on the forehead then move that same

hand on to the Thymus. Then, place the same hand over the heart and hold. Last, Retest.

4. If you are still having difficulty, then ask the statement: "This body is willing to give true and correct answers according to the will of God the Eternal Father, Jesus Christ of Nazareth and the Holy Spirit!" Do The Integration again. Then state, "I am willing ...." Perform the Integration and then say, "I am completely in the Light of Jesus Christ." Now retest and results should be accurate.

❧

SELF-MUSCLE TEST

1. Using a tall man finger and thumb, place thumb in center of tall man finger pad.
2. Think "yes" or make a truthful statement and all muscles are tight and strong. No slippage occurs
3. Think "no" or falsehood and the test will become weak and slip apart, usually with a snap release.
4. Place tall man finger of the left hand together making an "O" with very little tension. Place pointer of right hand in the "O" circle.
5. Think "yes" or truth, then try to push pointer finger out of circle. The circle will remain strong.
6. Think "no" or falsehood and pointer finger will break through circle with a gentle push.

❧

OTHER METHODS OF MUSCLE TESTING

1. The bicep bent at the elbow
2. The middle finger and thumb

3. The left hand middle finger and thumb in a circle with right hand middle finger placed into the circle and pushed against the contact where the finger and thumb meet on the left hand.
4. The thumb and middle finger of both the hands interlocked.

5. Pressure of right pointer over left Pointer

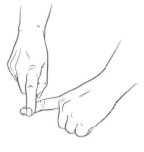

EXAMPLE

For an example, we will explain the steps of muscle testing using the bicep. However, any of the above muscles and others will respond to strength as truth and weakness as untruth.

ᬼ

Procedure For Muscle Testing

1. Establish a rapport with the participant. Ask **permission** to muscle test the arm.
2. Have participant **extend the arm** straight upward and out to the side.
3. **Stand** facing the person, slightly to the side, in front of the arm. Place two or three fingers on the arm near the wrist but not on the wrist or hand. Rest your other hand on his shoulder; this gives a feeling of **support**.

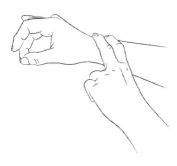

4. Have them breathe deeply and let you know when they are ready.
5. **SAY, "Hold",** wait 1-2 seconds, then push downward firmly but gently (about 1-2 pounds of pressure) and

have him meet your pressure to give a "holding" or,"locking" response. (Remind him that this is not a test of strength,)

6. Have them **say, "Yes"** – muscle test – the response you are looking for will be firm.

7. Have them **say, "No"** – muscle test – you are looking for the loss of energy indicated with a definite, even if slight, drop of the arm.

8. **Practice** the following to enable you to feel for clear "yes" or "no" responses. Say the words to the person as they give a response or as they repeat the words, as appropriate, as you test the arm.

"STRONG"	"WEAK"
• State your name	• Give a false name
• "Peaceful"	• "Boo!"
• "New shoes"	• "Dirty boots"
• Think of someone you like	• Think of someone difficult to like
• "Do my best"	• "Try harder"

9. **Explore together** other examples to see what makes the arm strong or weak. Both of you are getting the feeling of a strong or weak response. (Suggestion:

name some foods, see what the body likes.)

10. **Switch arms** to keep from tiring the working arm or bend at the elbow.
11. **Do not have eye contact** when the muscle is actually being tested.
12. **Use statements** rather than questions to gather information. You are speaking to the subconscious and it only identifies statements.

Communication will be clearer if statements are used rather than questions.
   "This workshop is the best choice for me." Rather than, "Should I go to this workshop?"

   If a MT response does not seem to confirm a truth response, search to uncover what is really being communicated. Keep making clarifying statements until you have collected enough information that you have an, *Ah-ha*, telling you this is the problem. Then work to resolve it.

C３

Troubleshooting

Here's what to do if something seems amiss or not correct in the muscle testing.

The purpose of muscle testing is to become more sensitive to the energetic responses within and to communicate with deeper knowing of the mental, emotional, and physical parts of either yourself or the person you're working on.

If a muscle test response does not seem to confirm the energetic response within, search with clarifying statements to uncover what is really being communicated.

1. Establish a rapport with the participant. Ask permission of them or of their spirit, if working in proxy, to muscle test. If they have physically/verbally asked you to help them, this is automatic permission.
2. Have participant rest his/her elbow on the arm of a chair and extend arm upward with palm of hand facing to the

floor, put tall man finger and thumb together.

3. Place two or three fingers on the top of the wrist.

4. Have the participant breathe deeply and put together the middle finger or pointer finger and thumb on both hands. This will keep the conscious mind busy. The conscious mind will take over and figure out all the answers if not governed. The conscious mind is task-oriented and a duty will keep it busy and out of the session, thus having access directly into the subconscious mind.

5. Push downward firmly, but gently, and have the participant meet your pressure to give a holding or locking response. Remind the participant that this is not a test of strength. Use a very gentle touch. As you practice this long term, your touch will become very sensitive.

6. Have the participant say their own name, then test the muscle strength. The response you are looking for is strength. The greater strength will manifest in the greatest, stronger truth.

7. Have the participant be false. Say a wrong name used as truth and as their

own real name. Test the muscle. You are looking for the loss of energy indicated with a definite, even if slight, drop of the arm.

8. To feel for clear "yes" or "no" responses, say statements to the person. They will respond or repeat the statements as you test the arm. Strong responses will come when you have someone correctly state their name or when you ask them to think of something positive. Muscle weakness will result when you ask them to give you a false name or to think of something that is not good for them.

    - Make statements of truth or false, muscle testing to know the answer from the sub-conscious.

    - If you are in question and don`t trust the answer, ask if *in the name of God the Eternal Father, Jesus Christ of Nazareth who died for us and who lives for us and the Holy Spirit if this answer is 100% true.*

    - If you get a double response, integrate and lay your right hand above and over the heart for just a few seconds. This will change the polarities and allow truth to manifest.

9.   If necessary, explore together other examples to see what makes the arm strong or weak. A suggestion is to name some foods to see what the body likes. Ask about sugar, "This body likes sugar." "This body recognizes sugar as nutritious for the body."

To summarize, once you have the muscle testing procedure down, all you need to remember is pray and Clear, then MT that the information they are testing for is accurate.

Tracking and Clearing Process

1. Pray: Connect with God and the Light.
2. Muscle test:
3. If the arm is strong, then go to Integration Procedure.
4. If the arm is weak, then go to step 3 below.
5. (Arm is weak in Step 2) Hold your Right Hand over the center of the heart for a few seconds. Muscle test (MT) again. The arm should be strong.
6. If the arm is still weak, hold right hand over the forehead then put the same hand on the Thymus and hold same hand over the heart.
7. You may need to do this several times.
8. Now muscle test (MT) and arm should be strong. Continue to Integration Procedure.

 C3

READY TO BEGIN

Now you are ready to find the breaks between the conscious and subconscious. **Use statements rather than questions** to gather information. You are speaking to the subconscious; and like a little child, it only identifies statements.   For example, "This workshop is the best choice for me," rather than, "Should I go to this workshop?" Without statements, you are asking two or more questions, and the sub-conscious doesn`t know which one to answer, or how.

Remember, the purpose of muscle testing is to become more sensitive to inner responses and communicating with and gaining a deeper understanding of the sub-conscious. The multiple parts: spirit, mental, emotional, and physical, are all examined closer with MT (muscle testing). As you develop this art, the sub-conscious will let you know the answer in your intuition before knowing the answer through Muscle Testing.   This makes the Muscle Testing a second witness of the truth of your inner-responses.

❧

TRACKING TO LOCATE 'BLOW OUTS' AND BREAKS

Tracking takes place after clearing. Tracking is finding your negative programs, beliefs, patterns, and feelings. These will manifest in your past and present energy programs where there is a pattern of past traumas. This is done by muscle testing and using positive statements with prayer continually. You may test strong and then have what is referred to as a "blow-out". This means there is a weakness identified and held in the muscles you are testing. Stop and work this out until the muscle system you are testing becomes strong again.

We are programmed from conception that when searching for answers, energy will go backwards in the physical to the oldest and deepest experience, belief or feeling expressed. This is what you are muscle testing for.

- Current age to 8 years.
- 8 years of age to one and if one is weak, switch to months down to birth (there are times you will count the months,

weeks or even days to find the exact day of the happening.)

- Fetal to Embryo development (there are times you will count the month or weeks in the womb or even days of conception)
- Conception - 12 days of conception (Hypothalamus is twelfth day)
- DNA Mother and DNA Father. At times you may need to count the generations.
- Twelve energy centers are counted as 1, 2, 3, etc. up to twelve which includes infinity levels of energy in each center
- Dimensions 1-12
- Other Worlds
- Other Universes
- Back to Infinity
- Erase this to point Zero and forever, never to be created again

When the arm stays strong, say positive affirmations.

Ask by MT, **"There is more to do."** If strong, you're finished. If weak, start over from the beginning.

Some find it helpful to **write down the levels where weaknesses are found**, as well as the responses to the following statements.

"We need more information." Making statements to identify exactly where the weakness has occurred can do this.

The body does have blocked energies. This is the reason for the weakness and only needs to be acknowledged as important, and then integrated for the issue to be finally resolved.

During the process of acknowledging and releasing, there is recognition of truth. Then the experience will be made clear.

They may cry and feel physical pain, yet have no conscious memory of what hurt them. Some may remember a sense or feeling.

They may hear, taste, smell, or visualize past events; and at times, there is tremendous pain.

Reactions to identifying weak MT vary greatly. The body is letting go of blocked energy and whatever happens, all is well.

♋

TRACKING STEPS SUMMARIZED

1. Clear Yourself, your space, and anyone you are working with (or they with you).

The importance of this cannot be emphasized enough. Our body's energy system is susceptible to influences most people will never see nor imagine. We need not fear. We simply need to know that to do this type of work, we need both to be cleared to the Light of our Savior Jesus Christ and then to be protected by His power. In this way, the only energy influencing the responses to muscle testing and the thoughts and feelings placed in our minds are from Christ and our own energy. This procedure is easy to learn. Do it sincerely, and it will be a blessing to your work, the angels will attend, and you will experience changes and growth that may surprise and delight you.

2. Identify Negative Patterns, Feelings, Beliefs and Programs. Write them down.

You may use the lists in the back of the book to find a "hot button" word, a physical ailment and the probable emotional causes, or simply observe any negative patterns that have reoccurred in your life. What is the feeling behind the pattern? What is the belief?

3. Write down the goals you want as affirmations (I am, I choose, I do).

This may simply be the opposite of the negative feeling you identified. It may be something you know is supposed to feel true, but doesn't, something like, "I am loveable," or "I am worthy of love and appreciation." Or it could be, "I am choosing friends and companions that are supportive and positive." You can use various sources to learn the language of affirmations. (See the free gift at the end of the book.)

4. "Track" where the negative program, beliefs, patterns, or feelings show up in your past and present energy.

This is the step where you find out where your energy "blows-out". You will be using the positive goal statements. Muscle test each of the levels listed below to see if that level remains strong when the positive statement (from #2 above) is said. If it stays strong, go on to the next. If it "blows-out" or the muscles weaken, you will ask and test a few more statements. Some find it helpful to write down the levels where "blow-outs" are found, as well as the responses to the following statement: **We need more information**

If YES -Test statements identifying how, what, why, when, and where. At times, it seems that the body's stuck energies and the reasons for their weakness, only needs to be acknowledged, then integrated, for the issue to be finally resolved. This is a process of acknowledging.

During this process, some people experience feelings of recognition. They may cry, or even feel physical pain, yet have no conscious memory. Some may remember or "see" past events, others may not. Reactions to identifying "blow-outs" vary greatly. Simply know that if there are reactions, they are a way the body lets go of blocked energy, and all is well.

5. Integrate

Integration is a process of gathering up old energy (the energy of the negative feelings, patterns, beliefs, and programs) you have just acknowledged by tracking, and "deleting it". There is now a void. With prayer, choose to replace those old energies with positive, new, and true beliefs.

This is a physical, emotional, mental, spiritual, sexual, prosperity process. To gather up the old energy, place your right hand over the forehead and then the thymus. (The right hand is the giving hand, and the thymus is the body's "reset" button.) Hold this hand over the heart. This tells the body it is time to dump the old energy, and it is "deleted". (At this point, some people physically feel the energy shifting and leaving the body. If this is the case, leave your hand there till the old energy is gone.)

Pray and ask that the program now change to positive (state your positive goal or affirmation).

Thank God for allowing the healing at this time, and for the assistance given.

6. Support your integration

After integrating, restate your positive goal as affirmations: ***I choose.... I am.... I do....*** Restate them as often as needed.

Believe that this healing is true and will be supported by God as you choose to support your own healing (and new beliefs).

Some people find it helpful to write their new beliefs/affirmations on a card that they keep at their bedside. Then for the next 21 days, they read it out loud morning and night, asking God for assistance and support in experiencing this new pattern in their lives.

Most of the time the changes are immediate. The words simply support the change.

ᘓ

TRACKING CHECK LIST

Track each; go into detail as needed…
(A complete printable tracking form with
space for notes is available to print at
www.BeLightAndShine.com)

1. CLEAR
2. TEST THE MUSCLE TESTING, CLEAR
   IT UNTILL IT IS CORRECT
3. IDENTIFY ISSUE The complaints,
   Identifying Themes, Identify the
   Primary Needs to be Addressed Now,
   Physical Ailments, Emotional Cause
   and New Positive Program of Truth
4. IDENTIFY THE AFFIRMATIONS to
   reinforce the work you've done.
5. TRACK:
   - Adult to 8 years
   - 8 years
   - 7 yrs
   - 6 yrs
   - 5 yrs
   - 4 yrs
   - 3 yrs
   - 2 yrs
   - 1 yr
   - Months 12 – 1 month:

- Birth:
- Fetus:
- Embryo:
- Conception:
- DNA Mother/Father:
- Generational/Ancestral:
- Cellular Memory:
- Energy Level 1:
- Energy Level 2:
- Energy Level 3:
- Energy Level 4:
- Energy Level 5:
- Energy Level 6:
- Energy Level 7:
- Energy Level 8:
- Energy Level 9:
- Energy Level 10:
- Energy Level 11:
- Energy Level 12:
- Other Worlds:
- Back Through Eternity
- Worlds
- Infinity
- Forever
- Point Zero, *("Please, God take it to point zero and erase it, or eliminate or uncreate it.")*

6. Integrate
7. Goal Review
8. Affirm Goal/ Positive input

Integration and Reinforcement

INTEGRATION

1. Pray and clear your space to God.
2. Identify the negative feeling and intensify it to the greatest degree you have ever felt it.
3. Tap with the right hand on the forehead and then thymus.
4. Put that same hand over your heart.
5. With your right hand on the heart, reprogram with positive affirmations using   I AM…. I DO…. I CHOOSE…."

REINFORCEMENT

1. Offer a prayer of thanksgiving.
2. Regular review of goal/affirmation
3. Review the goal and affirmations whenever you might have doubts the new 'program' is real.

YOU'RE INVITED TO JOIN THE

Be Light and Shine Community

ENJOY THIS SAMPLING OF WHAT THIS
COMMUNITY OFFERS...

Be Light and Shine Community

To begin healing at a deep level, the power of the integration in this book will jump start your healing.

Updated information, printable forms, cheat sheets, reference lists, new developments, special topics, exclusive courses and other alerts and a support group are obtained <u>with a Be Light and Shine Membership</u>

Printable Forms, currently available to subscribers of Be Light and Shine:

- Abundance ***Clear-ology*** Step by step checklist
- Tracking Form
- Energy Center Chart
- Integration Key Word List - Words that "Push Buttons" Reference List
- Feeling Word List to use to label emotions or to create affirmations
- Body Parts Checklist
- Clearing manuscript and cursive handwriting/print

- Clearing math symbols and numbers
- Clearing advanced math
- Feeling Words Reference List
- And more...

Membership information is found at
www.BeLightAndShine.com

**The writings that follow in this book
are samples** of what is available with your
Be Light and Shine Membership
1. Abundance Clearing Using ***Clear-ology*** –
   an excellent place to start integration
   work.
2. Water and Pre-Birth Programs
3. Brain Issues Associated with the
   Hypothalamus and the Central Nervous
   System

Be Light Abundance Clearing Using Clear-ology

Be Light and Shine **Community** Sample

Within each of us is an omnipotent power that will do anything for us if we learn to use it. The frequency of your word and vibrational change created by your word will make you believe this power is real. It has always taken care of you in many ways. It is the God-self within, our spirit or sub-conscious. This is *our power* when linked to God, it is everything. This inner energy, strength or power, when understood and used effectively, will make life full in every prosperous and abundant way. God and our Inner power want us to have everything! To learn in this life how to use this power within is enormous.

The Be Light method wants you to find the way *to* understand and know how to harness this power...hopefully, by learning to manifest your needs the rest of your life. If you had a boat, would you put it in a river with no rudder? When there is no direction, you are at the mercy of circumstances. Just like your boat with no rudder, you will always feel out of control.

Every thought and word has a vibration.

Change your vibration, Integrate.

Receive a new frequency and ask for the vibration of what you want. A like vibration is like a magnet. The same frequency will draw you together with what you are asking for and want to receive.

Here are directions for Muscle Testing (MT): Do Test the **A list** first. Say, "I am worthy." If it is weak, track and integrate. Now MT and do the rest of the list.

There are three lists A, B, and C.

The first **list A** is the first list to clear and integrate. This list will be used to clear **B**, and then **C**.

(A) BELIEFS AND PARADIGMS	
worthy	share
deserve	value/valued
accept	faith
I get to have	hope
receive	charity
give	moving forward with life

(B) SENSES	
feel	smell
touch	taste
hear	intuit
see	

(C) ENERGY IN THE PHYSICAL BODY	
Physical	Fight or Flight
Emotional	Limbic *(emotion and homeostasis)*
Mental	Neo Cortex *(sight and hearing)*
Spirit	Universe
Sexual	God and Prayer
No Pain	
Prosperity	

MT test each against A. In doing this, you will find many blocks holding you from your Prosperity and can remove them.

- I *FEEL* (list B) *worthy* (list -A). MT
- I am *worthy* (list A) **PHYSICALLY** (list B) to *receive* (list A).
- I FEEL (list B) *worthy* (List A) to MT (*all of the senses* – List B).

After clearing each list, this is how you proceed forward:

1. Make your list of things you want, or want to do. Keep the list in front of you. Read it two or three times a day.

    a. Clarify it with pictures. MT through every part of your picture wants against each word in list A.

    b. Then clear A list and C list against B. Integrate on every weak point. If it does not MT strong, do tracking and clearing, then Integrate (see example below).

2. Trace around each want or picture with your right pointer finger. This will take your wants and they will go directly into your brain. Keep your wants on your mind by using all your senses.

3. If you choose to tell others what you are working on, be prayerful and careful. Choose only those who will absolutely support you, or remain quiet and let the results speak for themselves.

4. Pray continually for what you want, keeping all channels open to God and the Universe.

5. Your spoken WORD creates the frequency of receiving. Be careful what you say because you <u>will</u> receive it. BE POSITIVE! Do Abundance Affirmations

❧

EXAMPLE

1. **MT List A, and clear each that need it.**
   a. I am WORTHY
   b. I am DESERVING
   c. I am ACCEPTING
   d. I GET TO HAVE
   e. I am RECEIVING / I RECEIVE
   f. I am GIVING
   g. I am SHARING
   h. I am VALUED / I have VALUE
   i. I am FAITHFUL / I have FAITH
   j. I am HOPEFUL / I have HOPE
   k. I am CHARITABLE
   l. I am MOVING FORWARD WITH LIFE

2. **Take the first word on list A, and MT each word on the B list with it. Then do the second word on list A with list B, etc.**
   a. WORTHY
      i. I am ***worthy*** to FEEL.
      ii. I am ***worthy*** to TOUCH.
      iii. I am ***worthy*** to HEAR.
      iv. I am ***worthy*** to SEE.
      v. I am ***worthy*** to SMELL.

      vi.   I am ***worthy*** to TASTE.

      vii.   I am ***worthy*** to INTUIT.

  b. DESERVE

      i.   I ***deserve*** to FEEL.

      ii.   I ***deserve*** to **TOUCH**

      iii. (and so on.)

3. **Next, take words on list A and MT each with all the words on list B** The Lists B and C are separated because at times, many issues on list C can be cleared up by clearing list B first. So be patient and do these in the proper order.

  a. WORTHY

      i.   I am **PHYSICALLY** *worthy*

      ii.   I am **EMOTIONALLY** *worthy*

      iii. I am **MENTALLY** *worthy*

      iv. I am **SPIRITUALLY** *worthy*

      v.   I am **SEXUALLY** *worthy*

      vi.   I am *worthy* of **NO PAIN**

      vii.   I am *worthy* of **PROSPERITY**

      viii. I am *worthy* not to live in **FIGHT or FLIGHT (to feel safe)**

      ix.   I am *worthy* **of EMOTION and HOMEOSTASIS (peace and harmony)**

      x.   I am *worthy* **of SIGHT and HEARING**

      i.   I am *worthy* **of the Truth and the Light** of God **(UNIVERSE)**

    ii.   I am *worthy* of connection with **GOD and PRAYER**

  b. DESERVE
    i.   I am **PHYSICALLY** *deserving*
    ii.   I am **EMOTIONALLY** *deserving*
    iii.   (and so on)

4. THEN Take the list A and the first word on list B and put it against List C
  a. WORTHY (A), FEEL(B)
    i.   I am *worthy* to *feel* **PHYSICAL**
    ii.   I am *worthy* to *feel* **EMOTIONAL**
    iii.   (and so on)
  b. WORTHY, TOUCH
    i.   I am *worthy* to **PHYSICALLY** *touch*
    ii.   I am *worthy* to **EMOTIONALLY** *touch*
    iii.   (and so on)

5. Combine the three words in whatever way you need so that you find any areas that need to be cleared and integrated.

*It is natural to have doubts. When this happens, get out your list and read. It will reestablish what you are doing and what this abundance ***Clear-ology*** is all about.

*The power within you does not argue, it simply does what you say. As you think and say it, the power within becomes stronger. It's like flipping your Light bulb switch to *ON*. The power is on and can also go out! It meets the frequency of what you want by the words you say. Your word put its Light arms around what you want and brings it back to you. At times it is given and brought right to your door step.

*Be thankful, be grateful! The enemy would want you to go into skepticism and non- belief. The reason would be to break your energy so you do not remain positive.

*Do not try to understand this or put limits on the amount. In your heart of hearts, just know it works.

*You can accept this or reject it. But if you want to move ahead in life, try it. You will like it.

Pre-Birth Programs

Be Light and Shine *Community* Sample

A YOUNG MAN TERRIFIED OF WATER

From the time of conception, the memoirs of this life begin. All that takes place in the mind and body is recorded as personal information, locked in the center of the brain complex, behind third eye or Master Cell. This is in the forehead and Corpus Callosum area, with the Hippocampus and Amygdale and Dendrites as extra storage for all of the memory that will accrue in life. Your entire existence is recorded here, not just this life. Praying for clearness and Muscle Testing (MT) will unlock what memories are there. Many of the fears we harbor are acted out in the present time as real in our life. They can come from perceptions in the womb.

Here is one of many true stories about the intensity of memory, proving the mind does record while in the womb.

⌖

THE STORY

A young man in his late twenties was terrified of water. When it rained, he would not go out of the house. If he was asked to swim or be in the hot tub, he would exhibit a nervous panic, refusing to be any part of it.

This nervousness was debilitating. He went into anxiety sweats, becoming so ridged he was unable to even move his eyes. If he tried to talk, he would stutter with broken words that made no sense. Checking by MT to find the age when the debilitating fear of water was recorded, it was found to be at six months in the womb! All his life had been lived with this immense fear as though it was taking place, *now*, in the present time. It was, but it wasn't.

His mother told the story of being in a boat with her husband out on the ocean. They were off the coast of Florida. She was six months pregnant at the time.

An immense storm developed and the boat capsized. Her husband drowned and she floated away on a round, white, donut shaped buoy. She hung on in wild waves, wind and raging water all night!

244

Many prayers uttered were for safety. They were answered as the current brought her closer to shore, rather than out into the ocean. All night she did not know where she was or what was around or under her. She was terrified that a shark might get her. All night she prayed for the safety of her unborn baby. At the crack of dawn, she could see the distance shore.

She paddled as best she could with her bulging tummy, bringing her baby boy to safety. She finally got close to shore, only to find she was in a swamp. Making her way through the swamp to shore, she was already terrified from the horrible night she had spent. Many hours in the dark she wondered if they would live, knowing her husband had not survived. But now, as sea plants wrapped around her legs, it was the fear of snakes and alligators, and the murky water. The safety of her baby drove her on. She did not know if she was even headed in the right direction. She went to what she thought was the shore.

It was raining when she crawled and clawed her way to the sand on the shore, exhausted! She could not move another inch. As she lay on the water's edge, cold and buffeted by the raging surf and rain, her thoughts were only of her baby. She hated the rain and the water that was causing all the fear and agony she was going through. She prayed again for her baby's life. She herself was very close to death. Then she slipped into unconsciousness.

A man who lived nearby was walking his dogs on the beach when he found her! He carried her to his home, then took her to the hospital. After several days of intensive care, she lived, as did her baby.

Her baby, now in his late twenties, still bore the scars of that long night in the water. His mind was stuck in all the terror created in his mind during that time when he lost his father and almost his mother. He registered all of the fear that his mother experienced on that horror-filled night. That night when he was six months in the womb registered as the base of his fears for over twenty years. He recorded the agony of losing his father and almost his mother, as well as all the shock of what water out of control can do. All of his own input, as well as all of his mother's thoughts and feelings, were now his present living programs.

He was able to release all the fear-based programs established in his memory while still in the womb. He now lives a normal life and is free to swim, but still won't go in the ocean. Swimming pools and hot tubs are okay. He no longer stutters and has processed the fears that made him ridged. He loves the rain, as long as it isn't violent, and is grateful God preserved his mother, with him in the womb, that long horrific night.

☙

THIS IS THE METHOD.

MT (muscle testing), intuition and tracking was used to find all of this information. If any other method had been used to help this young man, he would have been hopelessly trapped, living in fear and terror the rest of his life.

1. Discover: what, why, when, where and how by making statements and MT.
2. MT to get facts and a full understanding of what has taken place, collecting thoughts and feelings.
3. Track, counting backwards from 5 years old and Integrate as you find the fears.

4. When tracking in the womb, conception will need to be examined.
   a. Were there twins or multiple conceptions?
   b. Examine the feelings of when they realized the fear. Let them talk about it.
   c. Identify the deepest level of the fear or trauma. With this young man, it was fear of the loss of his own life, as well as his Mother's, because of water.
   d. Release him from the mother's tapes and programs with an Integration. It will be done by asking it to happen.
      "I now separate myself from all the fear programs of my mother at six months in the womb." Integrate.
5. Fill the void with positive affirmations.

Brain Issues
the Hypothalamus
and Central Nervous System

Be Light and Shine *Community* Sample

This is for Integration of brain function and the Hypothalamus. This will unite the *inner communications* of the central nervous system and connect it to the heart. It will repair the *beginnings* of memory loss. If the loss is great and the damage permanent, it will help but not turn it totally around. If caught early in its development, memory loss and the possibility of turning it around for health and healing is great.

This is for: ADHD, ADD, RAD, Anxiety, Parkinson's, Shaking, nervousness, Grief, Extreme Sadness, Depression, Dementia, and Dyslexia.

1. Left to Right mastoid over and back. Right to Left over and back. (Do both sides, Right and Left) MT for weakness in both directions.

 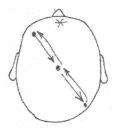

2. Right ear, over the top of the head to the left ear and back over the head to the right ear. MT for weakness. Integrate all weakness.

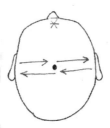

3. From the Third Eye (between the eyebrows), over the top of the head, to the base of the head (Cervical 1 down to Thorastic 1) and back over the head to the Third Eye.

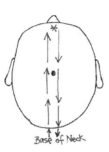

4. From the Third Eye, go Right around the crown of the head and back to the third eye. Then from the Third Eye, left around the crown of the head and back to the Third Eye. (Directly over the ears)

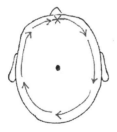 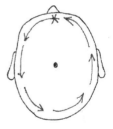

Integrate all weakness as you MT each direction over the center of the cranial and around the cranial, over ears to the Third Eye. If there is weakness, pray asking God to remove all debilitating programs and connect this area of the brain to the central nervous system and heart. Integrate.

Put your Left hand on top of head and Right hand on Thymus. "Think Light" as a "Prayer", ask God's Light to come through the top of your head and travel down through your body to your feet to complete this process. You will feel your body heat up with megahertz of Light flowing through you. Hold until it begins to cool. Remove your hands and affirm.

ᗧ

AFFIRMATIONS

- My brain is rewired to bring wholeness.
- I am balanced and whole from head to toe.
- My Present, my Past, my future, this moment, <u>now</u> all of my memory is excellent.
- Memory recall of every detail is perfect.

- I am remembering from head to toe, every movement.
- I always know where my hands are and all they do.
- I am connected to my whole brain with my hands, and my feet.
- I am remembering numbers and amounts. They stay in my memory, sorted and clear.

Please Accept These Gifts for You
to help you implement the information in this book.

Printable Forms and

Reference Sheets to support your

Implementation of the

Clear-ology Integration Method

Ↄ

Created for students and practitioners.

These Practical 'Printable Pages
can help support your success
*with the **Clear-ology** and Integration*
method of healing,
EVEN IF you've never done energy work
before in your life.

To receive your gifts, go to
WWW.BELIGHTANDSHINE.COM
And click on FREE GIFT.

⍒

HERE'S WHAT YOU ARE RECEIVING:

Printable pfd forms to use with yourself or others you help. These have been key for many starting this process. No referencing the book for instructions, rather, it keeps the process as smooth and useable as possible.

- Tracking Form with Space for Notes
- Feelings Words – Reference List to label feelings or write affirmations
- Words that Reveal Where to Work by "Pushing Buttons" – Reference List
- Clearing, Tracking, Integrating, Reinforcing Checklist
- ***Clear-ology*** – Abundance Clearing Step-By-Step Check List
- Printable Muscle Testing Instructions with Images
- Truth/Peace Agreement

Go to ***www.BeLightAndShine.com*** and claim your gift now to help you succeed at clearing out the old programs. Experience more peace and joy today!

THE AUTHOR

About the Author
Janet E. Taylor

How this all began...

I was badly hurt in a car accident. I was a passenger in the front seat of the middle car of a three-car wreck. It was before seat belts were mandatory. I was thrown out of my seat smashing my head into the dashboard and then into the ceiling of the car. I landed back in my seat, hitting the passenger door with my head and right shoulder hard enough to break the window. Another car hit us on the passenger side where I sat stunned. The momentum threw me across the car and into the steering wheel. I had no broken bones, but was hurt really bad! Every vertebra had been twisted and every muscle stretched to the maximum.

I was taken to the hospital and examined where they found nothing broken and sent me home to rest.

That evening the pain set in. I have never felt such excruciating pain. I didn't know that anyone could be in so much pain. I had given birth to four children but childbirth was nothing in comparison.

I was prescribed oxycodone pain pills to dull the pain. Within a month I was very much addicted to them. As I recognized my addiction, I threw away the pills I had collected and horded. I had prescriptions saved so I would never be without. I tore up all prescriptions and flushed! Luckily, they were gone; as had any been in the house at that time, I would have weakened. But I made it through!

I now take nothing for pain! I started dealing with the pain through my mind. This was the beginning of a great learning journey on how to govern my mind and body to overcome my pain.

One year after this accident, I was diagnosed with lymph cancer in the right side of my chest and my right armpit. The prognosis from the medical world was that I would die in six months or less. I didn't know what to do. Getting on my knees, I told God that my life was His whether I stayed on this earth, or left it.

Two days later, a lady I had met at an Amway meeting found me. I hadn't seen her for two years. My name had been on her mind so she decided to find me as she wanted to sleep that night. She was also curious, wanting to know what this was all about. I had changed jobs several times because I couldn't continue doing interior decorating. She searched work places I had been in and finally found me. She looked at me for a few minutes, then said, "I now know why I am here. I can tell you what is wrong with you. I can also tell you what to do." She proceeded to tell me that two years earlier she had been thrown out of a car window and hurt severely. She had gone to a naturopathic doctor who did cranial therapy. She also went to a dentist who did mouth splint therapy along with cranial therapy. She told me to do the same thing she had done and I would get relief.

I knew that God had sent her. I immediately picked up the telephone and called both doctors, making appointments. I worked with the naturopathic doctor for four and a half years. I had help from the dentist for about two years. Because I needed so much help, I was allowed to work for them to pay them.

As I started working for the N.D, I found that my earlier experience and knowledge of nutrition was an asset to him. He no longer worried about what was said at the front desk. If I had questions, I always asked him. My work expanded and I became a massage therapist, doing shiatsu, and myofascial release with cranial sacral therapy. I learned to do cranial therapy on my own head. I would pray, then and put my hands on my own cranial. God taught me what to do. I later took classes, but God was my best teacher.

I became a Hydro Colon Therapist (HCT). I realized that for me to live, I had to detoxify my body. Colon therapy was the quickest way to detoxify. It was then I comprehended the importance of emotional release. I realized I was always going to rebuild the same programs unless I learned to remove or change them in some way. Thus, I became a Certified Hypnotherapist and Neuro-Linguistic Programming (NLP) came into my life. Later, as a Master Certified Neuro-Linguistic Programmer (MNLP), I was able to help many people.

Up to that point, healing was back and forth. I would begin to feel better; then my body would go backward, growing the cancer again. When the cancer was progressing, I was very tired. Realizing it was the toxins in my body that made the tiredness and cancer re-growth, I had a hydro-colon therapy treatment every other day to take the toxins out. Along with this treatment, raw juices (mostly of a cruciferous nature and green with some carrot9 became my food of the day. This therapy was the turning point for me. Becoming a total vegetarian for thirteen years was also important, with no meat, sugar, cheese, milk products or anything white.

During all this time, I was working with people, teaching them everything I was learning. I found the things that worked for me also worked for them. I have been helping people ever since.

"The main learning: every illness and every problem in our body has an emotional capstone."

When I fully realized this, statement, the object of my search continually was that through prayer. God will lead me to the deepest capstone that I, or anyone I worked with had. This capstone, when found and removed, will help with a new level of healing and wholeness, then a balanced life.

I firmly urge, put all of your energy into knowing and understanding the life, mission and love of the Savior Jesus Christ, and you will find peace! Your life will change into a glorious experience, even though there may be hardship. Keep the course and you will be blessed, for He is the Way, the Truth and the Light.

49686843R00151

Made in the USA
Lexington, KY
23 August 2019